A
LENTEN
HOBO
HONEYMOON

A Lenten
Hobo
Honeymoon

Daily Reflections for the Journey of Lent

Edward Hays

FOREST OF PEACE
Publishing

Suppliers for the Spiritual Pilgrim
Leavenworth, KS

Other Books by the Author:
(available from the publisher)

Prayers and Rituals
Psalms for Zero Gravity
Prayers for a Planetary Pilgrim
Prayers for the Domestic Church
Prayers for the Servants of God

Contemporary Spirituality
The Old Hermit's Almanac
The Lenten Labyrinth
Holy Fools & Mad Hatters
Pray All Ways
A Pilgrim's Almanac
Secular Sanctity
In Pursuit of the Great White Rabbit
The Ascent of the Mountain of God
Feathers on the Wind

Parables and Stories
The Gospel of Gabriel
The Quest for the Flaming Pearl
St. George and the Dragon
The Magic Lantern
The Ethiopian Tattoo Shop
Twelve and One-Half Keys
Sundancer
The Christmas Eve Storyteller

A Lenten Hobo Honeymoon

copyright © 1999, by Edward M. Hays

Library of Congress Cataloging-in-Publication Data

Hays, Edward M.
    A Lenten hobo honeymoon : daily reflections for the journey of
Lent / Edward Hays.
        p. cm.
    ISBN 0-939516-43-8
    1. Lent—Meditations. 2. Picture-writing—United States-Miscellanea.
3. Tramps—United States—Language—Miscellanea.
I. Title.
BV85.H463   1999
242'.34—dc21   98-43672
                                                            CIP

published by
Forest of Peace Publishing, Inc.
PO Box 269
Leavenworth, KS 66048-0269   USA

printed by
Hall Commercial Printing
Topeka, KS 66608-0007

hobo art and cover design by
Edward Hays

1st printing: January 1999

Dedicated to

David deRousseau

A creative artist-vagabond
and good friend
with whom I have shared
the adventuresome hobo highway

Author's Acknowledgments

The image of a train on the cover of this book sets the tone for these acknowledgments. Thomas Turkle and Thomas Skorupa deserve credit for this manuscript being published rather than being permanently sidetracked. *Hobo Honeymoon*'s first incarnation was as a series of Lenten talks several years ago. The material has since undergone various reincarnations before being temporarily abandoned on a side rail.

Thomas Skorupa encouraged me to take the train of thoughts of this Lenten series out of mothballs and put it onto the fast track. Then he creatively breathed life and style into my manuscript. I am in his debt, for without his generous patience and his creative editorial skill, this author would have buried this book along with other dead manuscripts. My publisher, Thomas Turkle, has my gratitude for his encouragement to complete this book and for his creative labors in publishing it.

The Author

Born in 1931 in Lincoln, Nebraska, the author was a hobo from an early age. His mother enjoyed telling him, "Your first spoken words were 'Bye-bye,' and you've been on the go ever since." After high school he moved with his family from Lincoln to Kansas City, Kansas. Being restless, he soon ran away from home to the Benedictine Abbey of the Immaculate Conception in Northern Missouri. After eight years of college and theology studies there, he was ordained in 1958. For the next thirteen years as a priest of the Archdiocese of Kansas City, he camped out as a pastor in three different parishes. With a restless spirit in 1971, he left on a hobo backpack journey to the Near East and India. Upon returning in 1972, he camped out for the next twenty-three years in a cabin in a forest as the director of a contemplative prayer community, Shantivanam, near Easton, Kansas. The author presently divides his time between writing and being the priest chaplain at the Kansas State Prison in Lansing, Kansas. Rumors say that the old hobo hermit author keeps a packed bag under his bed, since he is again beginning to feel the old restless urge to travel on.

Contents

As a famous Christian hobo once said, "We must, to a certain extent, look for a stable port, but if life keeps tearing us away, not letting us settle anywhere, this in itself may be a call and a benediction. The world is understood and will be saved only by those who have no place to lay their heads. Personally, I ask God to let me die (metaphorically, at least) by the side of the road."

—Pierre Teilhard de Chardin

Preface:
On the Right Track

This simple hobo sign for a "train" christens this preface page with a prayer: May the daily reflections in this book help you to stay "on the right track" as you travel this holy season of Lent.

These Lenten reflections were written to help keep you from getting sidetracked by the usual distractions of daily life and to assist you in seeing this season's rich opportunities for inner growth. Lent is the annual *train*ing time for Christians, the ancient holy time of preparation as spiritual athletes. Lent is an extensive vocational training school for disciples of Jesus of Galilee.

Lent also has its own training table, with specially prepared meals, similar to the mess halls in training camps of athletes. Lent's training table, however, is for those who are striving toward the imperishable crown of which St. Paul spoke.

As a Lenten hobo, may you "ride the rails" aboard the Lenten Express as you travel this greatest of all adventures following Jesus from life to death to Life. If you wish to keep on the right track, simply follow the hobo signs that you will find chalked on the follow pages.

Clean Monday Before Ash Wednesday

The Eastern Orthodox churches do not observe Ash Wednesday. Rather, for them today begins the holy season of Lent. Traditionally on this day the faithful were to cleanse their souls by penance and to scrub clean their cooking vessels to remove all traces of meat and fat, which could not be eaten during this penitential season.

This can also be Clean *or* Clear Monday for you, a "Clear the Decks" Monday. That expression goes back to the eighteenth century when it was a naval command ordering seamen to prepare their ship for a battle. Clear the Decks Monday can be your preparation day to make everything ready for the beginning of Lent in two days. Take time to clear your mind and your agenda so that you can have space to engage yourself in the works of this holy season in a way that makes you a holier and more faithful disciple of Christ Jesus.

Cluttered decks, like cluttered desks and minds, make it difficult to be engaged in a great struggle such as the one facing us in the coming holy days of Lent. Our over-committed lives easily become crowded with projects and engagements that are booked days or even weeks in advance. On this Monday before Ash Wednesday, take time to clear your calendar for the activities of this season of reform.

This year, instead of some general Lenten wish, like, "I hope to make this a better Lent," be specific about your intentions. As with all significant life changes and personal reforms, it is essential to set both short-term goals (what I will do today) and long-term goals (what changes in myself and my behavior I'd like to achieve by Easter). These goals become a road map for the path of the coming forty days.

In making your Lenten Hobo Map, try to express your desires in a positive way, indicating what you wish to become instead of just what negative traits you desire to change. The age-old works of Lent are prayer, fasting and almsgiving. More recently, spiritual reading and the study of Scripture have been added to these. If you choose any of these traditional Lenten exercises, you may wish to include a short note on your Lenten Map about what you hope to achieve by each of these works. Be as specific, and realistic, as possible about what you can accomplish.

The following two pages have been provided for your Lenten mapmaking, but you may wish to create your own map, perhaps on the back page of this book. Whatever form your map takes, writing down your Lenten works is important since you can refer to them weekly to evaluate your progress. Moreover, the very act of writing them down moves a wish to an intention. Your map of intentions can then became a bugle call to action.

If the bugle gives an indistinct sound,
who will get ready for battle?

—1 Corinthians 14: 8

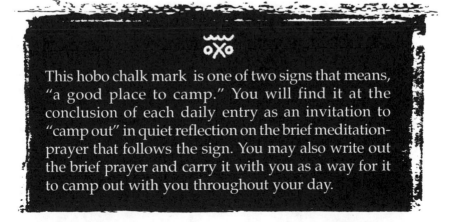

This hobo chalk mark is one of two signs that means, "a good place to camp." You will find it at the conclusion of each daily entry as an invitation to "camp out" in quiet reflection on the brief meditation-prayer that follows the sign. You may also write out the brief prayer and carry it with you as a way for it to camp out with you throughout your day.

Your Lenten Hobo Map

While being realistic about what you hope to accomplish, also do not hesitate to take some bold initiatives. Reflect on what activities might make this the best possible Lent of your life. As Ray Bradbury said, "Living risk is jumping off the cliff and building your wings on the way down."

Lenten Work   **Short-Term Goals**   **Long-Term Goals**

Prayer:

Desired Growth:

Fasting & Penances:

Desired Growth:

Almsgiving:

Desired Growth:

Other Lenten Works:

Desired Growth:

oXo

O Beloved One, give me your grace and strength
to perform these my Lenten works with great love and zeal —
and to do them one with you.

Mardi Gras, "Fat Tuesday": Overture to Ash Wednesday

Welcome, follower of Christ, to the curtain-raiser of your Lenten hobo honeymoon. While both the idea of a honeymoon and of being a hobo might seem inappropriate for the holy season of Lent, remember the words of the great patriarch Moses, who proudly declared, "My father was a wandering Aramean, and we were traveling vagabonds and vagrants who found our way to Egypt and lived there as aliens" (Deuteronomy 26: 5). Your spiritual ancestors were hobos, so rejoice in your proud heritage of traveling vagabonds as you begin these forty days.

"A hobo?" you still might say. "What an odd name for a Lenten traveler! I personally see myself as one of the zealous band of Christians preparing to go on a journey of forty holy days of fasting, penance and prayer, not a vagabond, tramp or bum!"

Ah, but hoboes are not bums or tramps! The origin of the word *hobo* is uncertain, but it begins to appear in the late 1800s and early 1900s as a name for migrating workers. At that time, wanderers — vagabonds — were put in three classes: "A hobo will work, a tramp won't, and a bum can't!" Bums were usually drunks and panhandlers. Tramps were shiftless; they worked some but also begged for their living. A hobo, however, was a migratory laborer who took on various odd jobs.

The word *hobo* is a contraction, like its cousin contraction *good-bye*, which is a short form of God-Be-With-You. Some believe that the first two letters, *ho*, come from the word *homeward*, and the last two, *bo*, are short for *bound*. According to the colorful history of this contraction, the original homeward bound travelers were wandering Civil

War veterans.

Another explanation says that the first two letters of hobo come from *hoe* and the last two from *boys*. Hoboes, thus, are those who used to hoe on the farm but now are on the road looking for other work.

Like them, you are a Lenten pilgrim preparing to take to the road — the road of reform and renewal on the way to Easter. And so you too could call yourself a Lenten hobo. You are a homeward bound spiritual migrant worker who is traveling beyond Easter Sunday on your way home to God.

God of all roads and ways,
remind me at every turn that I am homeward bound
and cannot truly rest until I find my home in you.
Fill me with zeal to be your holy hobo.

Ash Wednesday

Hoboes have secret signs, which they write in chalk on barns and fences to leave as coded messages to their hobo companions who might come along after them. An example of such a hobo sign would be this hieroglyph, which means, "Beware — bad dog."

At one time, that sign could well have been chalked on this Wednesday of grim fast and penance. Today, the "bad dog" of Ash Wednesday is toothless, not at all the threat it was long ago. Once, this Wednesday began forty days of serious, and I mean *deadly serious*, penance. It included a type of fasting far stricter than most diets today, embracing the absence of all life's pleasures and enjoyments. While recent reforms have given the Lenten season a more positive direction, and so have defanged this once-penitential holy dog day of Lent, Ash Wednesday remains a solemn day of fast and abstinence from meat, a day of prayer.

Traditionally, Lent begins not with a hobo chalk mark decorating the sides of barns or fences but with the sign of ashes marked on your face. Being marked with ashes is, in a way, a form of bodily decoration. That practice, which has a long history, can be observed in the contemporary practice of tattoos and body piercing. While bone and clay-bead decorations date back to around 26,000 B.C., the oldest form of decorating the body is with tribal markings and tattoos.

Today, we take up this prehistoric tradition and decorate ourselves with a temporary tattoo of ashes, a hobo mark easily removed. To avoid being told you have dirt on your face, you may be tempted to immediately wash off this mark of ashes. In the process, however, you wipe away your tribal marking as a Christian serious about the journey of reform.

What would your Lent be like if the mark on your forehead were made not with removable ashes, but with a forty-day dye? Then, each morning and evening when you looked in a mirror, you would be reminded that you are a Lenten hobo. Every time others looked at you they would see a marked person, one who is homeward bound for heaven as a Lenten traveler.

For our spiritual ancestors, the people of Jewish and other Near Eastern cultures, wearing ashes was a sign of mourning and lamenting. Ashes were usually associated with sackcloth, which was the clothing worn to mourn the death of a beloved or to lament a personal or communal disaster. In the early church, sackcloth and ashes were signs that marked the people who needed to do public penance throughout Lent, not just on Ash Wednesday. While ashes are still part of our Lenten tradition, what about sackcloth? If you are interested in reviving the use of this significant symbol, the following two pages show how to make a gunnysack scapular that can be your forty-day reminder.

O God, today may I often trace the cross upon my forehead as I say, "I am dust that will return to dust, yet in God I trust."

The Holy Sackcloth Garment

Originally sackcloth was worn as a full-length garment. The Old Testament has many references to occasions for wearing garments made from the rough, dark fabric used for grain bags; these were times of grief, mourning and penitence. Sackcloth was also worn as a garment of prayerful supplication for God to end some prolonged disaster, whether personal or national. Since the belief of that time was that sickness and misfortune, plagues or droughts were sent by God as punishment for misdeeds, sackcloth became a sign of penance for sin.

Sackcloth was also the symbolic garment of captivity and of prophets, since they usually foretold disasters as they called for a reform of life and a return to God. Moreover, because those begging for relief or pardon customarily wore it, this fabric became a symbol of humiliation.

Sackcloth was often worn as a secret undergarment, whose existence was only known — and felt — by the wearer (See 2 Kings 6: 30). Since the theme of Jesus' preaching was to reform one's life, we might wonder if he wore such a secret undergarment to keep him itching for holy reform.

A Lenten Sackcloth Scapular

Go to a fabric shop and purchase a small piece of burlap or gunnysack, the rougher the better. Cut out two squares of about three inches, or larger if you wish. Then tie, glue or sew two pieces of heavy cord to the top ends of your burlap squares. You now have a scapular, a mini version of an entire Lenten garment, which can be placed over your head so that one patch rests on your chest and one on your back. This Lenten scapular is best worn under your clothing as a tactile reminder that you are a Lenten pilgrim.

The following prayer is for blessing your homemade scapular and for investing yourself with the meaning of this Lenten symbol. After the prayer, you can trace the sign of the cross on your scapular and then kiss it before placing it over your head and shoulders. Each time you remove it to bathe, you can silently repeat this ritual as you put your scapular back on.

+ Blessing Prayer for Investing Your Lenten Scapular

O Lord of Hearts, bless this holy scapular
   so it will be for me a holy reminder of my Lenten journey.
the sign of cross is traced upon the scapular
May it remind me to be prayerful,
   generous with my gifts to those in need
   and faithful to my disciplines during these forty holy days.
May my Lenten sackcloth, the cloth of the poor and lowly,
   inspire me to be humble of heart.
As I wear this holy sign under my clothing,
   to be seen only by you,
   may it remind me to perform all my Lenten works
   for only you, my Beloved God, to see.

Ash Thursday

Besides ashes, Lent could also begin with a sign usually reserved for Valentine's Day — a red heart — painted on your forehead. This heart sign could be a reminder that these forty days are to be spent as a honeymoon.

The moon plays a very significant role in the celebration of Lent, for this is a lunar season whose date is determined by a special full moon. The celebration of Easter is always on the first Sunday after the first full moon following the March 21st spring equinox. The appearance of this spring full moon also determines the movable date of Passover.

Another special moon time is a honeymoon, the post-wedding holiday trip of newlyweds. In our modern busy world a honeymoon is no longer a full lunar month as it once was. More properly it should be renamed a "honey-half-moon," or for many even a "honey-quarter-moon," since the usual wedding trip lasts only one or two weeks.

Jesus frequently escaped from daily life, if not to the desert, then to deserted places to be alone in prayer. As one of his followers, even if you have a busy schedule, consider following Jesus by taking time in solitude to be alone with God. An actual desert will likely not be possible, but you can go into your bedroom, close the door and spend time alone with God. While a Lenten honeymoon retreat of a week or more may not be possible for you, consider at least a honeyday: one day out these forty days when you can be in solitude and prayer-communion. And if an entire day is not possible, then consider a half-honeyday.

So, rather than a formal wedding invitation, on this second day of your Lenten season you are given a red-hearted invite to a honeymoon, a romantic escape from business-as-usual. Today and throughout these forty days, strive to invest your prayers and spiritual works with as much love as possible. Since our prayers usually deal with practical concerns, consider adding to your daily prayer time devotional prayers that speak of your love of God. Such devotional prayers inflame the heart instead of simply involving the mind.

When seen as a honeymoon, Lent shouts out the great commandment, "You shall love the Lord your God with all your heart, soul, mind and body, and your neighbor as yourself" (See Mark 12: 30-31). It is fitting to spend these forty holy days as a hobo honeymoon. In the first place, regardless of our work or profession, we are all basically hobos doing odd jobs, just passing through this place we call home on our way Home. Secondly, we are working our way home as lovers, aware that loving is the greatest vocation.

This Ash Thursday is a day to realize that wherever you reside isn't your true home. Even Planet Earth isn't your real home. Home, rather, is where you came from — God! As you head home, see Lent not as some set-apart religious season but as a miniature mirror image of life itself. As a Christian, you are meant to journey through life as a disciple of Jesus. Yet to be a good disciple is hard work, if you're doing it right! It demands a life of prayer and great love as you continuously strive to grow more Godlike. This is a day to remember that growth always requires great energy!

Beloved God,
send your Spirit to fan the dead ashes of my heart
into flames of great love for you and all your creation.

Ash Friday

The sign for this Ash Friday, found under every Lenten Friday on religious calendars, is not technically a hobo sign. It is a Lenten hobo sign, however, since the symbol of a fish says a lot about how to set a course for the pilgrim journey of Lent.

Fridays in Lent are fish days! Traditionally, all of Lent is a special food season — yet more for what we *don't* eat as we observe fasting and abstinence. Fasting means eating less than a usual amount of food, and abstinence means not eating meat. In previous ages, both Fridays and Wednesdays were fast days, causing the Irish to speak of Thursdays as the day between the fasts. Gradually, Wednesdays were dropped as days of fast and abstinence, but until the middle of the twentieth century every Friday was a fish day of penance.

Those who fast for long periods are, of course, hungry. Jesus proclaimed that blessed are those who hunger — who hunger not for meat or food but for holiness and justice. True fasting is not a pious diet to lose weight, and true abstinence is more than substituting fish for meat — which is hardly a penance when many prefer fish for health reasons.

Consider fasting today — and each day of Lent — from apathy, the condition of a lukewarm heart, a zombie soul moving robot-like through religious and family duties. Apathy is the opposite of pathos, passion and devotion. Apathy is a creeping sluggishness of the spirit that comes upon us with the passage of time, yet it's a condition we can choose not to cultivate, a state of being from which we can abstain.

The cold, burned-out ashes of Ash Wednesday were a reminder of death, but apathy too is a sign of death. While the body may still be functioning, the soul and heart can float through life like a dead fish. On this Ash Friday, take the pulse of your soul, your inner life. Symbolically take your heart's temperature to see how warm is your zeal and enthusiasm. Ash Friday is Diagnose Yourself Day, an opportunity to examine the temperature of your prayers and spiritual works. If you and they are only half-alive, then begin to fast during these forty days from the hidden but lethal practice of apathy, and cultivate only a hunger for holiness.

Abstinence means more than absenting yourself from a good steak or hamburger; it implies absenting yourself from injustice. So, examine your personal and public life to see if you are presently supporting some form of injustice, even if only by your silent support. Lenten abstinence means more than cultivating a taste for fish or macaroni and cheese. Consider abstaining from apathy and cultivating a healthy diet of concern for the poor and needy or for those suffering oppression.

Examine your personal life for negative behaviors in your marriage and home life from which you can abstain instead of meat. Discipline yourself to enjoy an alternate diet of thoughtfulness and understanding, and nourish what fosters growth toward God and a generous heart. Examine your prayers to see if they are mostly about you, your needs and those of your immediate family. If so, then abstain from self-centered prayer and feast on concern for those who suffer from injustice. Begin today to remember in your personal prayers those persons who are exploited by large corporations that pay as low a wage as possible. Pray for those without health insurance, those who labor for corporations and chain stores that intentionally limit the weekly hours of their workers so they do not have to be responsible for employee health care.

 Abstain from meat today as a reminder, as Jesus said, to be hungry for justice. May this Lenten Friday fish sign be for you like an electric eel, a shocking symbol to awaken your conscience to the fact that there can be little growth in holiness without growth in a sense of social justice.

Ask yourself today, as a disciple of Jesus, if you're like a fish flapping its fins on the shore. Anyone who claims the title of Christian yet has no concern for those who are hungry, homeless and jobless is truly a fish out of water!

O God, regardless of what is on my plate today,
help me to feel the sharp pains of hunger
felt by those who starve for justice and equality.

Lenten Honeymoon
⊗tra Hobo Prayer

O Compassionate God,
   hear my soul's sad lament.
I am ashamed that my sorrow
   is itself so sorry,
so seemingly inferior and worthless.

Heal my poor words of sympathy
   when I say, "I'm sorry,"
for they are so limp and sickly,
   disconnected from real pain,
safely distant from personal suffering.

Any true communion of sorrow
   involves feeling sick myself,
suffering another's anguish,
   pain, sickness and loss.
Grant me, O God,
   a measure of such compassion.

My Beloved, give me the gift
   not so much to be patient
with those who are suffering
   but to be *a* patient
who suffers with the suffering.

Each of the ⊗tra Hobo Prayers in this book is taken from
Psalms for Zero Gravity by Edward Hays.

Ash Saturday

The Gospel reading for tomorrow's first Sunday of Lent tells of Jesus retreating into the desert. The desert was not only an arid place and a home to wild beasts; it was the place where God first made love to Israel after liberating her from the oppression and injustice of Egypt. Mt. Sinai's desert was the place of God's covenant or marriage contract with Israel. This Exodus was Israel's forty-year-long honeymoon with her Divine Lover.

The rich word *honeymoon*, some scholars believe, originated with a drink composed of honey and mead, a type of wine, shared by a bride and groom each night for a month after their wedding. For some poets the term honeymoon suggests that love after marriage, like the full moon at its peak, begins to wane — it grows smaller with the passage of days. The first lunar month of marriage was seen as the sweetest, being like honeyed wine. Israel's forty years alone in the desert with God was indeed a time sweet as honey.

When the Exodus ended and the Hebrews abandoned their years of migration, settling down in villages and becoming city dwellers, they quickly forgot about their marriage covenant with God. As happens in countless marriages, the honeymoon was soon over!

The prophets Isaiah, Hosea, Ezekiel, Jeremiah and others again and again called Israel to return to the desert. The prophet's call was not to embrace the desert as an act of penance or denial. Rather, the call of the desert was an invitation for Israel to be alone with God so they could again make love, so they could renew their marriage covenant.

To spend these forty days of Lent as a honeymoon might seem to be a contradiction in terms, for we usually think that Lent is about sinners doing penance and not lovers making love. Yet the moon herself is a Lenten nighttime reminder of this season's prophetic call. She grows smaller and smaller till finally there is no moon, symbolizing how our romance with God can slowly wane. But like the Lenten desert call to renewed love, the moon returns. After the three nights of darkness, the moon appears again as a slender sliver, then slowly grows larger and larger. As the moon increases, so can your love for God and others. The lunar season of Lent, then, can be a perfect honeymoon time for your love to grow larger.

As you prepare for the solemn beginning of Lent on Sunday, reflect on tomorrow's Gospel about how Jesus of Nazareth, led by and full of the Holy Spirit, goes into the desert.

Come, Holy Spirit,
usher me, as you led Jesus, into these desert days.
As the Spirit of Love, fill me so I can again
be romanced by my Beloved God.

First Sunday of Lent

Scribbled on the gateway to this first Sunday of Lent is the hobo sign of a cat. Decoded, this cat drawing means, "A kindhearted woman lives in this house," herein lives one who will be kind to a hungry hobo. Cats were holy symbols for the ancient Egyptians, but since the Middle Ages cats also have been signs of dark evil and the devil. Because cats and witches typically are constant companions, images of black cats abound round Halloween. In the Gospel of this day Jesus faces evil itself as he is tempted by the devil, and so the evil cat sign is chalked upon this Sunday.

In the desert the evil spirit tests Jesus as to the depth of his love of God. Rising out of the water after his baptism in the Jordan River, Jesus heard those beautiful words of God, "You are my beloved, upon you my favor rests" (Luke 3: 22). As we enter the desert of Lent as pilgrims on a hobo honeymoon, each of us can hear those same enchanting words of God, "You are my beloved." To begin this holy season as a spiritual honeymoon requires a new vision of Lent, once seen as purple penance for past sins. This new vision beholds Lent as a time of enhancing our love affair with God.

These forty holy days of renewal should be about romancing and enkindling our love for God with fresh passion and the enthusiasm of young lovers on a honeymoon. This view of Lent still allows for a sense of sorrow and acts of penance, especially if our relationship with God has grown cool. Although God never stops romancing each of us, it is possible to grow distant and unresponsive to God's ceaseless great love. Yet becoming aware of having a lukewarm heart can be a source of sorrow and the desire to reform our life.

The major work of a Lenten honeymoon is to improve our observance of God's first and greatest commandment, "You shall love the Lord your God with your whole heart, mind, soul and body, and your neighbor as yourself" (Luke 10: 29). Unfortunately, because this call is expressed with words like "You shall . . . ," it is often understood as coming from a solemn lawgiver. We might instead hear God simply saying, "Love me!" Hear in God's voice the same longing present in any lover's yearning to be loved totally by the beloved.

During his testing in the desert Jesus was given the opportunity to show how total was his love of God. In these coming days of Lent, you also will be given ample opportunity to show how much you love God.

Beloved God,
I pledge to love you more in body, heart and soul
so I can be found worthy of being called your beloved.

Monday of the First Week

Yesterday's symbol of a cat was seen from its sinister side. Today, we look at the sign of the cat as the positive hobo symbol of one who shows kindness toward those in need. Recall that the hobo's cat scribbled on a fence outside a house means that a kindly and generous person lives there.
The hobo cat is a sign for a person who is serious about one of the classic Lenten works: charity to the poor. Too often it seems that many people have negative feelings about social benefits to care for the poor and needy and those on welfare. The tendency is to divide those who are needy into the "deserving" and the "undeserving," with generosity considered fitting only for the "deserving" poor.

Jesus calls all of us to be generous to the poor, period! He turns over the apple carts of our middle-class values about charity to the needy when he says, "Give to the one who begs from you" (Matthew 5: 42). Hoboes put the cat sign on the house of a woman who would be kind to anyone who comes begging at her door. Similarly, a smiling cat can be the sign of a faithful follower of Jesus, who instructed his disciples not to judge who is deserving among those who beg for help.

A good Lenten penance, then, would be to write out that short sentence of Jesus recorded by Matthew about non-judgmental generosity to those in need; then put it in your wallet, pocket or purse. Like a hair shirt of old, allow the words of Jesus to prick your conscience into being generous to those in need. This act of sharing your wealth with the needy was once called giving alms. Whether it's named almsgiving or charity, it is both an act of justice and of love, since Jesus said that the love of God and the love of neighbor are one and the same. What is done to the least, the most outcast of his disciples, is done as an act of love to Jesus.

Ask yourself on this Lenten Monday if you are pleased or disturbed when your tax money is used for those on welfare. When your taxes go to the poor, are you pleased to be able to gift Christ, your Beloved, who is one with the poor, the homeless and those on welfare? During this Lent, and beyond Lent, begin to see every donation to the needy as a love gift to your Beloved.

If you did not include almsgiving among your works for these forty days, consider doing so now. Whether or not you have embraced the vow of poverty, consider taking the poor and homeless into your Lenten prayers. Other ways of giving alms to the poor include publicly speaking out for their needs and backing up your support by voting for candidates who promise to work to assist those in poverty.

*Lord, may I be ever generous to those who are in need
and never silent toward those
who condemn the poor on welfare.*

Tuesday of the First Week
Skinny Tuesday

A week ago today, Ash Wednesday Eve, has traditionally been called "Fat Tuesday" because of all the feasting, parades and parties that once preceded the beginning of Lent. The popular pre-Lenten attitude in the past was to brace oneself for Lent's long road of self-denial and sacrifice. Fat Tuesday was seen as an opportunity to extravagantly let loose one last time before having to tighten one's belt. It was a bit like a stag party before putting on the "ball and chain" of marriage. While we may look at both Lent and marriage a little differently now — perhaps focusing more on the honeymoon dimension of both — underlying the old notion of Fat Tuesday was a sense of preparation for the holy season ahead.

With your daily life so crowded with commitments and busyness, you may not have had an opportunity to properly prepare for this grace-laden season of Lent. But who leaves on a six-week vacation without advance planning, preparation and packing? Since Lent tends to jump out of your busy agenda like a surprise visit from the Holy Spirit, your Lenten observances can be a bit skinny. Yet even though we're at the end of the first full week of this season of renewal and reform, you still have an opportunity to examine your intentions for how you wish to spend these holy forty days. Such a reflection is essential, for a skinny Lent means a lean Easter. This Skinny Tuesday is a time to narrow down and focus on the priorities of your busy agenda to find what's really important.

A favorite rabbinical story of mine summarizes well today's reflection for all of us as holy hoboes on the road of life:

Once a traveler was passing through a Russian village whose rabbi was renowned throughout the land for his holiness. On the chance that he might see the holy man, the traveler stopped at his simple abode. He was shocked to see how bare and stark was the rabbi's room. It held only an old wooden table and stool, at which the rabbi sat prayerfully reading his scriptures.

"Rabbi," the traveler began, looking around the room, "where are your possessions?"

The old holy man looked up and returned, "Stranger, where are yours?"

Confused, the man replied, "Rabbi, I don't have any with me. I'm only passing through."

The rabbi smiled and said, "So am I!"

An excellent Lenten penance for this Skinny Tuesday would be to strive to make your personal life more simple. All of us would likely find this to be penitential because our countless commitments to family, friends, career and parish make life today so complex. Even our inner life, or prayer life, can easily become too complicated; so begin a Skinny Tuesday prayer-fast of making your prayers more simple and direct.

*O Beloved God, help me to use these Lenten days
to simplify my schedule by fasting from
being involved in too many activities.
May my Skinny Tuesday
resolution be to strive
in all things
to make it
simple.*

Wednesday of the First Week

In the desert, Jesus does find God, but he also encounters the evil one. As a follower of Jesus, you too should be forewarned. In your desert days this Lent, be prepared to find both God and the evil one, and be prepared, like Jesus, to be tested. As Satan asked Jesus to adore him, this holy season holds out the question: "Who, or what, do you adore: power, status, wealth or God?"

If we fail to see ourselves as hoboes, perpetually homeward bound, we may easily be tempted to adore other gods. If this life is seen as the end, how difficult it is not to adore power, status and money! Indeed, that temptation is present right in the fabric of our daily lives, especially, perhaps, in our work or career. Each day, our love for God and for those God has entrusted to us, is put to the test: Which do you love more, your loved ones, and Loved One, or the business of your life — even if it is "holy" or religious work?

Whatever your daily work, it involves more than making ends meets. The temptation is to find challenge, excitement and zestful enjoyment in your work at the expense of finding it in your marriage, family and love relationships. To meet this or any other temptations you will encounter this Lent, you can turn to the sign of the season, the cross of reform that was traced on your forehead a week ago. While the mark of ashes is no longer there, you need to ask if you are still serious about reforming your life. In your prayer today, ask God to enkindle a fire under any of your lukewarm loves, especially your love of God.

Remember the distinction between a hobo and a bum: A hobo is willing to work along the way, a bum is not. Anyone unwilling to work daily to make his or her loves vibrant and alive is a bum who only wants a free handout and refuses to work. We can be well-dressed bums, unwilling to labor at love, only looking for handouts, free gifts of love from others and from God. While true love is always a free gift given without any strings of hidden expectations, love is not free!

Love's first demand is for a response. True lovers are zealous in striving to make their responses greater than their gifts, but not because of any feeling of competition. By its very nature, love strives to express itself by giving more than is received. The test for every lover lies in how that lover responds to the commonplace gifts of love, for not responding to these day-in, day-out gifts is what makes a hobo into a blind bum.

A blind bum is one who takes any gift for granted, and the list of these for-granted gifts is long: from a good meal prepared at the end of a long day to rising refreshed after a good night's sleep. In your Lenten prayer today, include the petition of Jericho's blind beggar, Bartimaeus, "Lord, that I might see" (Luke 18: 41), so that you may be a grateful hobo-lover.

May my eyes be opened wide, O God,
and my heart opened even wider
with a loving thanksgiving for all my daily gifts.

Money Talks

"Money talks" is a favorite expression which implies that the voice of money is a voice of influence. So if you desire to influence yourself into making one or several major changes in your life this Lent, consider letting money talk to you.

Such significant changes can cost you as little as two dollars! To improve your life — which is the intent of Lent — think about making a contract with yourself that each time you fail in keeping a Lenten resolution, you will tear into little pieces two one-dollar bills!

I can assure you that such a penalty for being undisciplined will be painful, but it will also be very influential in helping you keep your Lenten resolutions. Whatever your goals for Lent, they will be easier to attain if you fine yourself two dollars each time you fail to keep an intention.

In the Gospels, when the woman broke a jar of precious anointing oil and poured it over Jesus, his disciple who kept the purse, Judas, was shocked and said, "What a terrible waste! Why was this precious oil not sold and the money given to the poor?" (John 12: 5). Likewise, you can be tempted to say, "What a terrible waste! Instead of ripping up my money when I slip and fail to keep a Lenten resolution, I'll give the two dollars to the poor." I assure you, while that is a worthwhile thought, giving the money to poor or the church will not pain you as deeply as destroying your two dollars — for money talks.

In a letter written in 604, Pope Gregory the Great said of the Lenten law of abstinence, "We abstain from flesh meat and from all things that come from flesh, such as milk, cheese, eggs...." Naturally, this would include butter. For almost a thousand years this was the norm for Lenten abstinence. Butter was easy to abstain from in lands where olive oil was available for cooking, but in Northern Europe giving up butter was a difficult discipline. In some areas, exceptions to the no-butter rule were permitted if one gave alms in place of not using butter during Lent. Because of this practice one of the richly endowed steeples of the French Cathedral of Rouen became known as the "Butter Tower."

Personal change is always difficult, and you may be tempted to soften the pain of reform and kill two birds with one stone: You can excuse yourself from a resolution and give alms at the same time. In the process you may even become the benefactor of your own personal "Butter Tower." Always keep in mind, however, the goal of Lent: the conversion/construction of a new you is a far more valuable monument. So, consider the influential "two dollar" practice as a way to reform your life.

Jonathan Robinson, a psychotherapist, proposes the creative two-dollar penalty for self-change in his book *Instant Insight*.

Thursday of the First Week

 Jesus came to a crossroads in the desert, where he would be tested on which road he should take. One road led to becoming a disciple of the devil, and the other road was the way of being a true son of God. The Good Hobo Jesus, after his baptism, was led into the desert by the Holy Spirit to firmly commit himself to the right road in his life. It would be a homeward bound road, but not one that would lead back to Nazareth and his former life. The Spirit guided him along the road that would lead to the cross. So, today, you may also be tested at a Lenten crossroad. For as a Lenten hobo traveling these forty days, you will come to many crossroads, many places of decision.

Deserts are favorite military testing grounds for new weapons and secret airplanes. Lent is such a desert testing ground, and the same evil spirit who tested Jesus will visit you — with a full arsenal of potent weapons and secret plans. Again and again you will be enticed to choose power or convenience over your covenant with God. You will also be tempted to compromise your Lenten practices. However, do not fear. Remember how in his desert testing ground Jesus proved he knew which was the right road, and he remained faithful and loyal in his love of his Beloved. Do not fear, but instead rejoice, for the very same Holy Spirit that led Jesus into the desert is at this very moment leading you.

Since Lent has many crossroads, ask the Holy Spirit always to lead you along the right road. Yet not all Lenten choices are between good and evil. Today you may be standing at a crossroads, a fork in the road. The road sign that points to the right has a grim skull and crossbones painted on it. It points the way of the old traditional Lent of forty days of fasting from things you enjoy and of doing penance for your sins. This purple road of sorrow and guilt for sins calls for heroic self-denial and discipline.

The other road sign points to the left, and on it a flaming red heart is painted. It points the way to forty days lived as a honeymoon rather than a gloomymoon. If you take this road you are called to travel it with great passionate delight as you perform countless deeds of love. Be forewarned, however, for this road leads you over a cliff; you may "fall" in love again with God and with yourself, your spouse and with life.

Who shall say which of these two roads is the best for you? Both roads have their own holy history and mystical traditions. And even if you try to combine elements of both Lenten ways, one way will inevitably be your primary path. One way will be better for you, even though it may not be better for another person. Yet do not be anxious about how you will know which road is for you, for God has given you the gift of the Spirit of the Holy as your guide. You only have to ask your Spirit Guide which road you should travel.

Yogi Berra, the baseball hero of famous one-liners, once said, "If you come to a fork in the road, take it!" So take either Lenten way, but take one of them with a passionate desire to travel it with the greatest of devotion.

Holy Finger of God, point me this day in the holy way.
Whichever path I take, may it strengthen and deepen
my love for you.

Friday of the First Week

 The sign of the fish is again upon this Lenten Friday, a sign of penance and denial. This Friday looks forward to Good Friday and the death of Christ Jesus on the cross. For him it was the end of the road, a dead end.

When Jesus first took up the desert road upon which the Spirit led him, the final end of that road was hidden from view. Three years later, the road he chose would lead up the hill of Calvary to his death on a cross. It was, indeed, a dark Friday, and, for us, a *Good* Friday.

You may be old enough to remember traveling the Lenten road of the pre-Vatican II church, which was primarily a way of penance and self-denial. If so, you may find that old purple penance road more comfortable because it is so familiar to you. For those born after 1960 and the Second Vatican Council, this has become a season of preparation for new converts' reception of Baptism and full initiation into the church. Moreover, for post-Vatican Catholics, this new Lent is a *via positiva*, a positive way, and is focused on renewal instead of repentance.

For those living in the northern hemisphere, both Lenten roads pass through the season of spring, so that at the crossroads of the old and new Lents is the meeting point of penitential purple and spring green. At this juncture both roads can be penitential — both provide an opportunity to experience the sorrow and remorse pointed to by today's fish sign. The greening rebirth of creation in spring during these Lenten days can be a creation sign of renewing your heart and expanding its boundaries. Spring is a season of growth, yet allowing your heart's boundaries to grow larger can also be penitential. Similarly, thinking of others first, and their needs and feelings, is an act of loving self-denial. Expanding your Lenten heart can be a communal as well as personal journey — and a shift to such a communal perspective can be truly penitential. This expansion of boundaries challenges all of us to move beyond any rigid concepts of who does or does not belong to the Body of Christ — and such a shift of faith can be penitential. Being personally accountable for your own holiness and spiritual growth, instead of leaving that responsibility to your pastor or other "experts," can be penitential.

Whether you're traveling along the purple or the green path, Lent offers many opportunities to embrace the fish sign of self-sacrifice. If, rather than the above "green" type of penance, the denial of things you usually enjoy will assist you in the real work of renewing yourself and your baptismal discipleship, then practice such Lenten works with zeal. Know that either Lenten road taken with a full heart will lead you to the same place that Jesus' road led him — up the hill of Calvary. Yet to die to yourself is to be on the road to life.

On this Friday, Jesus' death day,
may I be one with him who died for me
as I join him and die to all that is unloving in me.

Saturday of the First Week

Today ends the first full Lenten week, a week marked by the hobo sign of the cat. This is a day to remember Jesus' advice to his disciples when they fasted and did works of penance. They were not to "look like something that the cat dragged in." The prophet of Galilee was opposed to wearing the sad face of self-denial.

The smiling cat in this week's hobo sign symbolizes a housewife's happy reception when a hobo comes to her back door for a handout. Jesus likewise called his followers to be happy hypocrites — to put on a happy face — whenever they were fasting. The reflection for this Lenten day calls us to remember the Master's stern warning about keeping our Lenten works and penances so secret that only God sees them. Then, lest we perform them simply to be rewarded, we might go a step further and try to hide them even from God!

As Jesus continued his teaching, he could well have said, "When you fast and deny yourself, don't look like the cat that ate the canary!" He did not want his disciples to be like the fat-cat Pharisees, who were smug and self-satisfied with their spiritual practices. He knew that any disciplines or works undertaken for self-satisfaction take us on a detour from the homeward bound road that is the way of Lent. Moreover, because such selfish acts make us smaller of soul, they will always be less than what we could have done and thus can't take us all the way "Home."

As we well know, the classic discipline of this season

is fasting. For the first three centuries most Christians prepared for Easter by keeping a fast of only two or three days. Then this fast was extended to include the entire week before Easter, today called Holy Week. By the fourth century, Lent had grown to the present forty days. Some believe the practice of monks fasting for forty days, in imitation of the desert fast of Jesus, deeply influenced this Lenten tradition.

Today's cat reflection calls us to look at what makes fasting really effective. Do our fasts keep us moving, hobo-like, along the homeward path by leading to the kind of fasting that Jesus favored? Are we moved off course by our desire for reward or self-satisfaction, or does our fasting make us hungry and thirsty for justice? Jesus' type of fasting leads us to feel the pangs of hunger not so much in our stomachs as in our hearts. It creates an ache after justice for those cheated by society, by fate and the life-conditions in which they were born.

The fasting that is pleasing to God occurs when our hearts fast from being smug and content with the level of justice available toward all people starving for justice. It is to know the hunger for dignity and acceptance of those whose steady diet is discrimination and hate because of their race, religion, sexual orientation or social class. Contemplate today's hobo image and make part of your prayer on this first Saturday of Lent the desire to put on a happy housewife face and heart as you fast and give of yourself.

*O Gracious God, I lament that my love for you
is not greater, that my good works and love
are so meager: Help me do better.*

The Second Sunday of Lent

 In the Gospel story on this second Sunday in Lent, Jesus takes his closest disciples and goes up a mountain to pray. While in prayer, the Hobo Jesus is transfigured and in the process is given a foretaste of his final destination and glory, as he is homeward bound via Jerusalem and the way of Calvary. On a large rock on this transfiguration mountain-top, Simon Peter could have scribbled in chalk this hobo sign, which means, "a good place to camp." Peter is ready to pitch a tent on the spot so as to continue to live in this religious experience.

In the midst of his prayer Jesus has a mystical experience and enters a state of altered consciousness, his body and even his clothing shining with the splendor of the sun. He and his three friends enter into the bliss of another state of reality; no wonder Peter wishes to remain there. Jesus reminds his friends, however, that he is a hobo who can't camp out on that mountaintop but must first suffer and die before his transfigured reality becomes a permanent one.

Jesus climbs a high mountain to pray, going apart from the usually noisy crowded conditions of his village to be in communion with his Beloved. We know from the Gospels that he frequently took these mini-honeymoons, brief retreats that echoed his forty-day desert rendezvous with God. Rather than going to the village synagogue, or even into a closet to pray in secret — as he had instructed his disciples in the way of prayer — today he ascends a mountain. In doing so, Jesus imitates Moses, who desired to be alone with God on Mt. Sinai.

"Remember you are dust and to dust you shall return" — this was how Lent began. Now Jesus in his mountain prayer hears God say, "Son, remember you are fire and to fire you shall return." Jesus knows he is homeward bound to again become blazing light, for his human flesh, while indeed dust, was once stardust! His life, and yours, is a homeward bound journey from dust and ashes to light!

Scientists estimate that over one hundred million meteors enter Earth's atmosphere each day! As they streak through our atmosphere, these meteors burn up and turn to ash or dust. It is estimated that every year over four million tons of stardust fall to Earth. The particles of dust on the table next to you could be as old as our solar system, some four and a half billion years old!

A good Lenten reflection would be to find some dust nearby (which if your living room is like mine shouldn't be difficult), and run your finger across it. Look upon that dust and reflect on where it may have come from. Then gently touch the flesh of your hand and be filled with awe that the atoms in your skin and flesh are made of stardust. Know that like Jesus you too will someday shine in splendor greater than all the stars and that today you are homeward bound to glory.

O dust of my being, remind me where you have come from and thus ease my fear that my dusty flesh will never glow again.

Monday of the Second Week

Your Lenten hobo honeymoon this week calls you to the strange practice of using profanity — in imitation of Jesus of Galilee. Shocking, but true! While the usual definition of profanity is wicked or blasphemous speech, its root is the Latin word *fanum*, which means temple or sanctuary. When *pro* is placed in front of *fanum*, it refers to what takes place outside of or in front of a temple.

So how did Jesus use profanity? The Gospels relate that he was frequently absorbed in prayer and imply that he lived in a continuous state of communion with God. Most of the ceaseless prayer of Jesus took place outside the temple; he even made it a point to visit the most profane areas of life. So when he was in conversation with his Abba, Jesus would most likely have used profanities, the common language of daily life.

Jesus also told his disciples to pray without ceasing, which seems impossible since daily life demands so much of our attention. Most of us find it much more difficult to pray outside the temple, but praying constantly requires using profanities, words spoken not in church but in the secular space of daily life.

A good Lenten exercise would be to experiment with using non-churchy words in your daily prayer as a way to find a more natural and constant prayer-communion with God. Take a little time and reflect on a few of your most frequently used words and expressions as starting points for your prayer. What would your profanity prayer sound like?

Personal prayer and attending religious services inside a church are among the most popular and effective Lenten works. Prayer is encouraged during Lent with different special devotions that become part of the usual

 parish schedule for this season. Yet the hobo sign, "a good place to camp," is written not just on your parish church but on your home, workplace, farm, town, city or wherever you happen to be temporarily camped. And just as your church has a special language that can help lead you into prayer, each of these profane "campgrounds" has its own language that you can use to create new prayer forms. So experiment praying today with common, daily secular words as your profanity prayers.

Give me a Lenten tongue, O God,
to use common speech
in my words of prayer
to help me pray constantly to you.

Tuesday of the Second Week

Since prayer is a major Lenten work, today is a good time to begin addressing the questions: "How should I pray?" and "Why should I pray?" One immediate reason for you to pray is that you are a hobo! Life is a journey that requires a passport, and as a wandering vagabond you carry a unique passport. The writer of the letter to the Philippians reminds us that we are not really citizens of the United States, Canada, Australia, England, France or any other country, but rather that "our citizenship is in heaven" (Philippians 3: 20).

Perhaps along with the gift of holy ashes on the first day of Lent, you should have been given a small blue passport book with the word "Paradise" stamped in gold on the cover. To carry such a passport would help to remind you that you are homeward bound in this season of Lent. Unlike Christmastime, in which most every street is decorated with lights and symbols of the season, except for the occasional large wooden cross draped in purple cloth outside a church, the road of Lent has no such reminders. To be a Lenten pilgrim in our secular society is to be both a hobo and an alien.

And why should we pray during this sacred season? Prayer is perhaps the best reminder that the pilgrimage of Lent is really a journey of love. In fact, prayer is the passport that gives us entrance to the honeymoon lands of communion with the Divine Lover. A honeymoon is a lovers' holiday trip, in which the couple can easily be identified by how absorbed in affection they are for each other. That image gives us a clue as to *how* we are to pray. For prayer is not some form of heavenly taxation or obligation; it is an exchange between lovers. During this Lenten hobo honeymoon, strive to recapture the romantic spirit of young lovers on a honey-sweet holiday.

Most of us are at least a little uncomfortable with this image of a loving God. *Lover*, itself, is not an easy word to use; spoken in public, it sounds almost like a profanity. Seldom do a husband or wife refer to one another as "my lover," and it usually seems an even more inappropriate word to use for a friend.

Let Lent encourage you to be more like Jesus, who was intimate with God, his Lover, throughout his journey to Jerusalem and all along his life pilgrimage. Like the Master, constantly use the passport of prayer to transport you along the honeymoon journey of Lent.

I'll let you in on a little secret: God loves to be called "Lover."

O God, may I find secret pleasure in being your lover this day.
May I know hidden, intimate joys in honeymooning with you,
my Beloved.

Wednesday of the Second Week

There's a story about an absentminded professor who left on his honeymoon but forgot to take his bride! If you have remembered to take your Beloved along on your Lenten hobo honeymoon, then God should be rarely out of your sight or out of your mind and heart. Like young lovers on their honeymoon, you will travel with your Beloved not out of any sense of obligation, but out of joyful delight — for joy is the sign of one who is homeward bound. With this Companion at your side, the sky becomes a sacred blue traveling temple of God, and everything under the dome of this temple becomes holy space.

This Lenten Wednesday gives us an opportunity to learn from the teacher from Galilee, who loved to sneak away and be alone with God all along his journey up to Jerusalem. Roman Catholics speak of stopping at a church in the middle of the day to "make a visit," to pray and be with God who dwells within. To simply walk inside a church or shrine can make us feel different. Being inside any sacred space or structure, simply by our silent presence in that place, has a deeply prayerful quality.

All of Lent can be such a "visit." As you journey through this day, rub your eyes frequently as a prayer ritual, or frequently make a small sign of the cross upon your eyelids, as you pray, "Lord, that I might see" (Luke 18: 41). Ask to see your world and the entire cosmos as a *fanum*, a temple. Were your eyes to be so Spirit-gifted, they would not be blind to the actions of your daily life as holy prayerful rituals performed inside the temple of the world.

When you daily view the world as God's temple, you do more than visit God, you constantly rub shoulders with God. Being aware of living and working in a cosmic holy temple will challenge you to treat every person and everything with great reverence — just as you might treat holy ministers and sacred vessels at your local church or cathedral. Moreover, anyone who handles all of life with reverence is someone who is praying constantly.

Any reflection on prayer can invoke a sense of inadequacy, since few if any of us feel we know how to pray. When prayer seems difficult, you might desire to seek some reliable resource on a method for prayer. There is no shortage of manuals, books and pamphlets on prayer — they could fill a hundred libraries. Gurus and spiritual teachers also abound, eager to teach you how to pray.

You might reflect today on how Jesus learned to pray. Did his mother or father teach him? Not just his daily Jewish prayers, but who instructed him in how to pray profanities, those prayers lifted up to God from outside the temple or synagogue? Who taught the teacher from Galilee to pray always, to be in constant communion with his Beloved Companion?

Just like my skin, may I today be enclosed in prayer,
surrounded by — clothed by — a living, breathing prayer.

Thursday of the Second Week

Yesterday the question was raised: Who taught Jesus how to pray? This Thursday reflection proposes one possible answer: The desert and mountains were his teachers — and they can also be yours! You might object, "But I don't even live near a mountain or a desert!" Even so, if you desire to learn from these prayer teachers, you might reflect carefully on this prayer by the thirteenth century Persian Muslim Sufi mystic, Jala en-Din Rumi:

> Does anyone write upon a written page?
>   Does anyone plant a sapling in a place already planted?
> No, one searches for a paper free of writing,
>   sows a seed in a place unsown.
> Be, O my friend, a place unsown, a white paper
>   untouched by the pen.
> Return from existence to non-existence.
>   You are seeking your God and you belong to God.

This book uses several hobo signs as Lenten symbols, and the two pages following this Thursday reflection are a sign of how to begin to pray. They have been left entirely blank, empty of any printed word, "untouched by the pen." Take a minute or two and meditate on them, soaking up their empty whiteness.

One of the first steps in learning how to pray is to create within yourself this same kind of white space. Notice that the pages are completely empty of words, even holy words. Some might say they are "wasted pages," yet such empty space is the foundation upon which rises the shrine of prayer. It is even the topmost spire of that shrine.

After presenting the various worries and concerns of your prayers of petition to God, try to empty yourself of those cares, as well as your plans for tomorrow or memories of yesterday. Such empty space at the end of prayer gives God a chance to have the last word. And to those who might warn, "An empty mind is the devil's workshop," you can reply, "An empty mind is God's playground!" For God's creative play always completes our work more fruitfully than we could ever imagine.

In the midst of his busy ministry, with the thousand and one demands made on his time and energy, Jesus frequently went off to a mountaintop or desert to pray. Even more than in Jesus' day, white silent space is an endangered species, and many seekers go in search of it in lonely places and monasteries. Yet silent space is not restricted to special places or to a special few contemplative souls. The excellent spiritual guide, Anthony de Mello, tells this brief story: "Once an easygoing disciple complained that he had never experienced the silence that the Master requested. Said the Master, 'Silence only comes to active people.'"

The wise Lenten hobo takes advantage of experiences of being "trapped" in empty and unproductive space. These are occasions when you're forced to wait at a restaurant, on the phone, at a stoplight. When you find yourself in such a place, don't become upset. Instead, take a deep breath and enjoy the vacant space as a white desert oasis that's ideal for contemplation. As T.S. Eliot said:

The desert is not remote in southern tropics,
the desert is not only around the corner,
the desert is squeezed in the tube-train next to you.

You can make this "empty" profanity prayer into desert prayer as you pray in a doctor's waiting room, standing in a checkout line or stalled in a traffic jam.

Come, Beloved God; write boldly on the white page of my heart those four shocking, scandalous words, "You are my lover."

Friday of the Second Week

 Today is another fish day and so a good time for a story about a prime home for fish, the Pacific Ocean. Anthony de Mello tells a tale of an ancient island a mile or two offshore that had a great temple with thousands of bells. Whenever the wind blew, the bells, in unison, would peel out in awesome clarity and grace. Over the centuries the island sank deep into the ocean, yet a legend arose that if someone listened carefully the temple bells could still be heard in all their beauty. One young man sought the mystical experience of the fabled bells and spent weeks and weeks trying with all his attention to hear them. Yet all he heard was the wind in the palm trees and the endless sound of the surf. Frustrated, he gave up all his exercises to empty his ears and decided to go home. Before he departed, however, he decided to lie on the beach and enjoy the sand, the warmth of the sun and the sound of the endless waves. In the depth of his relaxed silence, he unexpectedly heard a faint tinkling of a bell, then several bells a bit more loudly, until finally he could hear all thousand bells in all their splendor. To his amazement, the young man was swept away in wonder and joy.

This fish story suggests another form of profanity prayer: striving to listen to all of daily life's non-temple sounds you can hear. Such a profanity prayer can be aided by the abstinence prayer of this Fish Friday. Just as the Lenten exercise of not eating meat can assist in cultivating an appreciation of simpler foods, abstaining from hectic noise today can help you enjoy a meal of listening to life's ordinary sounds. Fill your plate with the sound of the wind and the hum of your computer, the song of birds and insects, the sounds of traffic and the laughter of children at play — and in all these sounds hear God.

Abstinence prayer calls for a cleansing of the ears not so you can hear temple bells in ordinary, profane sounds, but so you can hear the quiet voice of God. Fast from radio and TV today, not because they are empty of God, but so you can hear God more clearly in all the sounds of life. This avoidance of noise is a good penance for this season, yet such abstinence prayer is really no penance at all for a lover of God.

Jesus had a religious experience while in prayer on the mountain of the Transfiguration, and the young man in the story had a graced moment while relaxing on the beach. God gives such special gifts not as some kind of religious treat for being holy. Religious experiences are only doorways from one state to another. They're intended to be passageways and not living places. As we saw with the disciples on the mountaintop, they are not places where Lenten hoboes are to camp out.

On the other hand, you may have dismissed the possibility of a religious experience in your life, thinking that such gifts are only for a few selected lovers of God. On this Fish Friday, however, consider this haunting saying of the fifteenth century Muslim mystic, Kabir: "I was surprised when I heard that the fish in the ocean are thirsty."

Empty my ears, O God, of the thunder of my many thoughts and the roaring of my busyness so I can clearly hear your voice.

Saturday of the Second Week

The mountains and deserts have always been among God's favorite places for a *rendezvous*, French for "a lovers' meeting." The word literally means, "present yourselves." In that literal translation is an excellent instruction on how to pray. It is certainly the one that Jesus used: Simply present yourself to God, who is present wherever you are.

God is everywhere: in the desert, on the mountain, in the marketplace and in your home! You have only to "present yourself," as fully as possible to the Mystery of the Divine Presence. On this Saturday, practice presenting yourself as best you can to each passing moment and see if you hear not bells but your softly spoken secret name, "My lover."

One of the main understandings of Christianity is seeing Jesus of Nazareth as the beloved of God and, as such, unique in all of history. Remember too that Jesus called you to follow him, and, in his pattern, to do so as a beloved of God. A dynamic tension exists between the two names, *beloved* and *sinner*. It may be hard, especially in the light of the purple penance of Old Lent, to continue to see yourself as a beloved one at the same time as you see yourself as a sinner — but that dual reality is also at the heart of Christian belief.

Saturday is the Sabbath day, and so today provides a good opportunity to look at some of the Jewish Hasidic masters' great insights into prayer. One thing they said was it is a great wonder that we should be able to draw so near to God in prayer, for there are so many walls between God and us. Even though God fills the world, God is also so very hidden. Yet these masters offered hope when they said that a single word of prayer offered with great devotion can topple all the walls and bring us close to

God. Just one word of prayer filled to overflowing with deep love has the enormous power to remove all the barriers between God and us.

This second week of the Lent will end tonight at sundown, so renew your desire to make this the best Lent of your life; renew the Lenten resolutions you wrote in your Hobo Lenten Map. This Saturday also looks forward to Jesus' Gospel story of the unproductive fig tree, which will be the focus of the third week of our Lenten hobo honeymoon. Thus, a tree is a good closing image for this week.

While life is usually crowded with concerns and worries, don't plant your tree of love in a forest of Anxiety Elms or Deadline Project Poplars. Don't root the tree of your prayer amidst the dense thicket of troubles and problems. Instead, take your Lenten Lover's Prayer Tree and plant it in the wide open prairie of the closest — even if it's the smallest — empty space. After planting your tree, sit under its welcoming branches, for there you may have a rendezvous with your Lover.

O God, may I present myself to you in a loving way
in the midst of my every activity on this Lenten Saturday.

Third Sunday of Lent

The hobo sign that begins this new week of Lent is the hobo way of saying, "Tell a pitiful story!" This coded sign on a fence or tree outside a house indicates that a compassionate person lives there. In today's hobo honeymoon Gospel reading (Luke 13: 1-9), Jesus gives us a garden parable about a fruitless fig tree, which the orchard owner wants chopped down because it is unproductive. The gardener tells a pitiful story as he pleads for the fig tree's life, saying he will hoe around it and manure it.

Jesus' parable today answers the question, "What is the world's oldest profession that is today's most popular hobby?" As you may have guessed, the correct answer is being a gardener! The profession of gardening goes all the way back to the beginning, when God the Gardener created the first garden in Eden. God, who loves cooperative ministry, shared that holy work by making Adam and Eve partners in gardening.

Heaven's garden name is paradise, which comes from the Persian word for the enclosed royal gardens of their kings. Gardens and religion were early partners: Egyptian temples were surrounded by gardens, and the Chinese had their sacred grove-gardens. Even the mini-gardens of potted plants in ancient Greece became small shrines in honor of Adonis, the god of growing plants. In the northern hemisphere, since the Lenten season and the spring season accompany one another, the thoughts of many turn to their gardens and yards during Lent.

On other levels, gardening is one of the primary works of Lent; it's at the heart of your hobo journey of return to the Garden of Eden. As we saw early in this book, the word *hobo* may have originated with the hoe-boys, the sons of farmers who left the farm and were on the road in search of work. These hoe-boys were not bums or tramps and would work hard at any odd job, including digging up a spring garden plot.

Lenten hoe-girls and hoe-boys, how does your soul garden grow? In the garden of your soul, are the trees rich with fruit or are they barren? The tradition of Lenten "gardening" is centuries long, rich in its heritage as a springtime retreat. While recent reforms of the season have been very positive, even a causal look at the daily involvement many of us have given to Lent tells a pitiable story. Often we've taken the easing of Lenten restrictions as an excuse to let our soul gardens go to seed. Today's garden of Lent is overgrown with the weeds of overwork at our jobs, full social calendars and other secular activities, busy school events, demanding sport practices and games to attend, or even the endless round of evening TV. Examine your soul garden today for any weeds that need to be hoed out so that good plants can grow and bear a rich harvest. This Sunday, take time to lovingly examine your inner life, especially your prayer trees and alm trees. Make sure they aren't barren and sickly from neglect.

With renewed love and devotion
may I care for my soul garden, O God,
as I gently remove the weeds and nurture the good plants.

Monday of the Third Week

The childhood rhyme, "Mary, Mary, quite contrary, how does your garden grow?" plays in the wind on this Lenten Monday. Indeed, how does the garden of your life and your soul grow these days? This purple season of Lent is also green-thumb season for all of us as hoe-boys and hoe-girls. It is prime time for the kind of spadework that can provide fruitful, healthy plants. Yet if we look back to yesterday's parable of the fig tree, we realize that there's also a sense of urgency in the air. When the gardener finished his story that evoked pity from the orchard owner, he added that if the tree didn't produce fruit after this year's hoeing the owner could then cut it down.

How quickly the days of Lent are passing; this is already the third week. On this Lenten Monday, examine how faithful you have been to the Lenten disciplines you embraced on Ash Wednesday. The human tendency is to delay change; for most of us *tomorrow* is the best day of the week to change and reform. St. Paul, however, tells the Corinthians that Scripture, like many of today's commercial products, carries a warning label: "They (Scriptures) have been written as a warning to us!" (1 Corinthians 10: 10).

Paul used the example of our Jewish hobo ancestors: They soon grew bored with their desert wandering days and fell away from God, suffering as a result. Jesus spoke with great urgency about the need to reform our lives because the domain of God had arrived. This Lent should be saturated with the same sense that "now" is the time; do not delay taking seriously your spiritual life.

Does that message fall upon deaf ears? Our hearing may indeed be dulled to the urgency of that message if we believe that we have another life secure and available in a safety deposit box. The potential power of Lent is in its reminding us to wake up to the reality of life; this is our opportunity to cultivate our soul garden. "Remember you are dust and to dust you shall return" — now is the time for hoeing!

The hobo sign, "Tell a pitiful story," could be chalked over many a conversation in our culture, since it is so commonplace to bemoan the problems and difficulties of life. It seems that those who fail to season their conversations with problems and difficulties are considered to be out of touch with reality. It is thought that only the simpleminded aren't constantly beset by problems. Yet we often use our moaning to keep from having to deal with our problems. There's a story about a traveler in the Missouri Ozarks who stopped at a general store, in front of which a hound dog sat howling its head off. The traveler asked a man standing outside the store, "Why's that hound dog howling so much?" He replied, " 'Cause he's a'sitting on a thistle." The traveler asked, "Well, why doesn't he just sit somewhere else?" "Well, friend," the man said, "it's 'cause he'd rather howl!"

Our prayers can also be pitiful story-conversations with God, simply howling about life's thistles. As we move into this third week of Lent, you may be tempted to tell God a pitiful story that because of your work, your obligations, your problems and your difficulties, you are prevented from cultivating a healthy spiritual life. If you are so tempted, be forewarned: Instead of a kindly reassuring pat on the back, God may ask you a question, "Did you use the pain, failures and unsavory circumstances of your life as manure to fertilize your garden, or did you only complain about the 'crap' of your life as a way of hiding from problems?" Now is the time to cultivate and fertilize.

"Waste not, want not" — Today, may I make this old saying new, as I ask your help, O God, to not waste these Lenten days.

Tuesday of the Third Week

The gardener's offer to manure the barren fig tree in Jesus' Gospel parable suggests another name for this purple Lenten season: the Forty Manure Days. Yes, Lent is manure time. (The color and smell of such a season is left up to your fertile imagination!)

Originally, to manure meant to till the land, to engage in the everyday activity of farming. In fourteenth century England, the word *manure* referred to the "common work," the daily labor of ordinary people. And in America until the twentieth century, the common work of the majority of people was manuring, tilling the land. Although it is estimated today that only about 5-10% of us farm as a profession, this season of Lent remains a time for all of us to manure.

These Lenten manure days are the time to fertilize your prayer garden, your love relationships with God, family and friends. They are also days to cultivate your love, your charity-justice, to the poor and needy. Charity-Justice should always appear as a Siamese twin, joined at the hip, for all charity is but the sharing of good things with those who in justice are entitled to it.

The word *manure* evolved from meaning the act of spreading fertilizer to now referring to the fertilizer itself. Remember, Lenten hobo, that the hoe of this season's spiritual disciplines can be useful in spreading the manure that will fertilize your life and prayer. Be aware too that nothing is so rich a fertilizer for your life garden as "crap," a folk term for all those foul-smelling realities like failure, sickness, personal inadequacy and interpersonal problems. The word *crap* entered our language from the colorful Old Dutch word *scraps*, which meant, "excrement" and also "fertilizer." Pain of all kinds should be medically treated whenever possible, but even physical pain can be useful as manure. Rather than telling your spouse or co-worker or God a pitiful story, embrace as fertilizer for your soul garden the pain of your life that cannot be removed.

Manure can come in all shapes and in a thousand varieties. It might come as mostly decomposed past wounds or as fresh foul-smelling crap. Whatever the kind of manure you might handle today, instead of looking around for some place or way to dump the unpleasant things of your life, consider using them as fertilizer for your soul garden.

O Divine Orchard Owner,
may I cleverly use any manure that's dumped on me today
as fertilizer to help me grow in holiness, hope and happiness.

Wednesday of the Third Week

Even if you are a post-Vatican II Christian, there are pale ghosts of Old Lent that continue to haunt this season. These ghosts materialize as religious drill sergeants wanting to flog flabby souls into shape. They carry harsh tools for spiritual improvement: the whip of penances that lash soft soul flesh and the gaunt belt-tightening daily practice of strict fasting.

Hoe-boys and hoe-girls have another Lenten tool and symbol to place next to the great sign of the cross: the common garden hoe. If you have one in your garage, you might want to bring it inside your home and put it in your prayer corner. You can even tie a purple ribbon around it so it will be recognized as a symbolic Lenten tool for working the garden of your heart.

Recall that hoes are also the tools of hobo migrant workers. A Lenten hoe in your home can remind you that these days are not so much about penance for past sins as about reforming yourself. These are hoe days for turning over the soil of your soul garden, for reworking the soil of your marriage, profession and vocation as a homeward bound vagabond.

As any gardener will tell you, good soil is essential to a good garden. Good soil, not too wet or too dry, is also critical to the flowering of a good marriage and a good spiritual life. Hoeing, in turn, is essential for good soil by allowing the nutrients of the manure to be absorbed into the ground. Hoes are ideal tools to keep weeds controlled and to stir up the soil to keep it moist. Hoeing allows the soil to breathe by breaking up the hard crust, letting the grace of life-giving oxygen work its way in. So, as you can see, a hoe in your home can be an excellent symbolic Lenten life-improvement tool.

Still, you might object, "I live in an apartment and don't have a garden, much less a hoe. So I find it difficult to relate to all this talk about how to care for soil!" Be aware, however, that in your family history, perhaps not that far back, your relatives worked the soil, if only in a backyard garden. Let those buried family memories awaken and allow you to see the significance in this new Lenten symbol.

Today's reflection began by looking at the harsh, painful penance tools of the Old Lent. If you feel a need for some good old Lenten pain, consider hoeing around your checkbook or pocketbook! Prominent among Lent's traditional works is almsgiving, and while this section of the Lenten garden can produce the most beautiful fruit, its soil is often most resistant to being worked. How easily does a stone-like crust form over the money in your purse or pocketbook, hardened by the idea that your money is yours and not simply loaned to you. Take your Lenten hoe, with its sharp edge, and feel more than a pinch as you dig deep to give generously to some charitable cause. Lent calls you to give move than mere token gifts from your surplus but to lovingly give with generosity.

English author Donald Nicholl quotes the Jewish Talmud, "'The son of David will come only when there are no coins left in one's pocket,' and 'Religion is about money: how to give it away.'"

Holy Gardener, may I hoe out the weeds of greed and selfishness
so that the beautiful flower of generosity
may bloom in my soul garden.

Thursday of the Third Week

The earth's hard crust can prevent the moisture of spring rains from soaking into the soil. Likewise, your relationships with others and with God can become crusted over by the tamp, tamp, tamping of routine and the passage of time. Knowing this, the gardener in Jesus' parable story proposed hoeing around the barren fig tree to break up the hard crust so that it might bear fruit.

What creates the hard crust over the soil of your soul garden? What prevents your inner life from breathing freely? Is it routine — repeating the same things day after day — that causes a crust to form over your relationships with those you love? Is it the repetition of the same prayers and rituals that allows a hard crust to form over your personal relationship with God? If so, on this hobo honeymoon Tuesday, gently hoe around the plants of those relationships and carefully introduce a new pattern of relating, a new way of communicating or a new prayer form to let your love breathe.

Besides breaking the crust of the soil, hoes are useful to remove weeds. Weeds are the enemies of a good garden, for they choke healthy plants and drink up the moisture plants need to flourish. Weeds also tower umbrella-like over a garden, blocking out the sun's rich rays from reaching the good plants. Your Lenten hoe is a symbolic tool for removing those weeds that choke the young plants of reform and renewal that are eager to grow. Unlike a spade, a hoe, used correctly, doesn't injure the young plants of virtue or holiness in the process of removing the weeds. As you gently take up your hoe, however, remember the nature of weeds, especially if you're tempted to call them wildflowers.

You can easily practice a form of self-deceit by sparing

wildflowers that are in reality vices. The following is an abridged list of common weeds that are often renamed as wildflowers:

1. The weed of a lack of commitment can be renamed a "free spirit."
2. The weed of selfishness can be renamed "taking care of old number one."
3. The weed of the absence of prayer and worship in daily life can be renamed "liberation from religion and the church" or "My work is my prayer."
4. The weed of cynicism that grows questions like, "Why vote?" or "Why be honest?" is often renamed the wildflower of "reality" — "That's the way it is."

Consider examining your soul garden to find your own variety of such wildflowers that may be trying to hide from your hoe.

O Divine Gardener, may I see the weeds in my garden,
and with a holy hoe may I remove them gently but firmly.

Closing the Gap Day

Dr. Benjamin Mays, the President Emeritus of Morehouse College, believes that everyone can reach the level of greatness. He defines that seeming unattainable goal as follows, "Wealth, position, or power are no measure of greatness. Greatness is defined by what we have become and what we might have been. The people who close this gap we call great."

Lent is the gap-closing season in which you first realize what kind of person you can be and then make real efforts to become that person. The resolutions you made at the beginning of this season of renewal and reform are gap-closers. As such, they have a life far beyond these forty days.

The French writer Leon Bloy said the greatest sadness in life is to not be a saint. Regardless of how successful and talented you may be, if you fail to become that unique, one-and-only, fully alive person that God created you to be, then how sad it is. Lent as a holy season challenges you to aspire to be as Godlike as possible in forgiving and loving. We've all heard how the average person actualizes very little of his or her potential mental powers; the same is true of our spiritual potential. Lent as a holy season challenges you to reach for that potential, to aspire toward the greatness of soul that comes from cultivating virtues like justice, mercy and love.

To desire to become a saint, not the plaster type with a halo, but someone who desires to close the gap between who he or she is and what God has gifted him or her to be, is a great adventure. The following parable by Anthony de Mello speaks of this exciting venture:

> The core theme of the Master's teaching was life. One day he told his disciples about meeting a pilot who flew laborers from China into Burma to work on building jungle roads during World War II. It was a long flight, and so to pass the time the laborers spent hours on end gambling. Since they had little or no money to gamble with, they gambled with their lives. The rule was that the loser had to jump out of the plane without a parachute!

> To that the Master's horrified disciples said, "Oh, how terrible!"

> "True," said the Master, "but it made the game exciting."

> After they had spent some time pondering his story, he said to them, "You never live so fully as when you gamble with your life."

This is almost the middle of Lent — and it may be past that in your life journey. Why not start now to play the exciting game of becoming a saint?

Friday of the Third Week

 This Lenten Friday is another fish day, and a good day to recall that fishmeal makes an excellent fertilizer. Abstaining from meat on this Friday not only can remind you of the denial of this holy season, but choosing a fish meal today can help fertilize your Lent.

Friday fish are special; they are holy fish. Long ago the old English word for a flat fish such as sole or flounder was "butt." This kind of fish was often eaten on holy days, and so the flounder became known as "holy flounder" or "holy butt." In time it evolved into "halibut," the name of a familiar fish today.

On this Friday, whether you eat halibut or tuna, see the fish on your plate as holy. Let it be a reminder that all days of Lent are holy days. In contemporary society, which allows a world completely naked of Lent to flood easily into your home and life through television and other media, such frequent reminders as holy fish are helpful.

On Good Friday, Jesus' death on the cross fertilized the world with his love and sacrifice. The fish was among the most recognizable early Christian symbols for Christ, and in some places in the apostolic church, rather than bread and wine, bread and fish were used for Holy Communion. So fish on Fridays can also offer a unique Eucharistic reflection. As Jesus fed the multitude with fish and bread as symbols of the heavenly banquet, you might consider celebrating similar simple Eucharistic meals in your home on these Lenten Fridays.

May your fish meal today be a type of Eucharist, a

communion with Christ the Fish, who gave himself up to nourish each of us and who by his death cross-fertilized the world with life. As his follower, what you eat today calls you likewise to be fishlike and to fertilize your daily world with love and generosity.

O Jesus Christ, Holy Fish, who died that I might live,
help me fertilize my world that it might be fully alive.

Lenten Honeymoon
⊗tra Hobo Prayer

O Holy Wisdom Teacher, instruct me,
    for I wish to be your eager student
in the cosmic chemistry class of conflicts
    and their secret creative power.

I've failed to fill my life's test tube
    with my problems and challenges,
desiring to conduct my experiments
    with only the simpler substances,
like happiness, success, pleasure and the promise
    of a string of bright, sunny days.

Thus failing to test my trials and crosses
    for hidden gifts of gratitude and wisdom,
I have failed to tap into a valuable resource
    containing great life-energy and creativity.
Help me today, Master Teacher,
    to be a better chemist in your art of love.

Saturday of the Third Week

Compost that is made up of kitchen scraps, leaves, grass clippings and other organic discardables is another form of rich fertilizer. Lent invites you to begin a compost pile that can serve you not simply for these forty days but throughout your life. Often problems in life can be like smelly garbage; when set aside for awhile, they can become good fertilizer to nourish your life and your loves. Prayerfully placing a difficulty in a symbolic compost pile allows for the kind of chemical reaction among the various elements that can transform a situation. It provides the kind of distance that is often needed between a painful event and your ability to use that misfortune to work for your good.

Take care, however, for it is possible to keep the stinking garbage of life around not in order to make rich soil, but simply to dump it on others and even on yourself. Such use of the garbage of life falls under the hobo sign, "Tell a pitiful story." Indeed, it is difficult not to dump on others when we feel we have the weight of the world — especially all its compost — on our shoulders.

The good news is that God gives each person just an acre in life, a small plot in God's domain. At the final judgment you will not be asked if you saved the world or even the church, but only, "What did you do with your acre?" So, hoe-girl or hoe-boy, take your hoe and use it to mix the daily compost around in your little acre. Begin to make it a personal Garden of Eden.

To do this, you might start by seeing in your small plot the same kind of ground upon which Moses stood in front of the burning bush when he was told to remove his sandals. See your life's acre as holy land. "Take off your shoes" and be astonished, be in awe.

From that sacred ground you can begin to embrace fully the challenge of letting your acre bear the fruit that will produce an abundant harvest. Lent reminds us that soon it will be Harvest Time, another name for our final Homecoming. For Lenten hoe-boys and hoe-girls, the joy of Easter at the end of Lent is an appetizer for the Great Harvest Festival, the Great Hoedown. As in that American folk celebration, that boisterous, square dance festival often held at harvest time, there comes a time when work hoes are laid down. So, take advantage of the hoe time you have been given.

The hoedown is also a reminder of your death. Soon it will be time to lay down your hoe, plumber's wrench, computer — or whatever your tool of work — and rejoice in your personal final harvest. Heaven can indeed be a hoedown, where you are swept up into a great dance and party, for you have done a good job with your acre. God will look at your life's harvest and say, "Well done, good and faithful gardener."

May my Lenten works bear a rich harvest for me and the world, for far-reaching is the redeeming power of every holy deed.

Fourth Sunday of Lent

Decoded, the hobo chalk sign that marks this fourth Sunday of Lent means, "a well guarded house." The implications of such a warning sign are many and ominous if it is chalked on your house, your parish church, or especially your heart. It's only natural to be concerned about the physical safety of your home, but what happens when such concern becomes excessive or when it spreads to your heart?

Jesus tells us a beautiful parable today (Luke 15: 1-32) about a young man, a hobo, who must have feared that he would see just such a sign on his father's home. In the parable, the brother of this prodigal son would certainly have placed such a hobo sign on the gate of their home. The parable is a wonderful Lenten story about a young man who leaves home as a hoe-boy and returns as a hobo. The nameless prodigal son becomes the patron saint of hoboes and of all Lenten pilgrims. (This uncanonized saint, St. Prodigal Son, would make a marvelously welcoming name for any new parish or any church discussion group. Yet I wonder how many Christians would be reluctant to be associated with a church or group so named.)

From the earliest times, the focus of Jesus' story has been upon the forgiving, "prodigal" father. I use prodigal to describe the father too since its second dictionary meaning is to be excessively *generous*. The first definition, of course, is being excessively wasteful, as his hoe-boy son was with his inheritance. Often overlooked, however, is the truth that the black-sheep son can only come home because he has left home — in the process wasting his inheritance — while the good, hard-working, homebody brother can't come home since he never left it. The older brother questions his father's love for him, while his returned hobo brother *knows* of the fullness of his father's love, which is both unconditional and lavish. The parable, as Scripture scholar Robert Funk proposes, is a teaching of Jesus not only about the generous pardon of the father, but also about the homecoming that only comes by leaving home. Jesus never asked a follower to do anything he hadn't done or wasn't willing to do. He required his followers to leave family, home, village and occupation and, like himself, to become a homeless person, one who had "nowhere to lay his head" (Matthew 8: 20).

You are homeward bound, even if you are presently "camped out." You may not, like most hoboes, be camped out under a railroad bridge but rather in a house on a boulevard or in some apartment, yet on one level you are no less homeless. Your real-life prodigal sisters or brothers along with real-life hoboes make excellent spiritual guides for traveling the road back home. Hoboes make good Lenten teachers in the school of how to live simply. These vagabonds are often shown carting their few belongings in a bundle tied to a stick they carry over their shoulders. Being literally homeless, they can remind you also to see yourself as homeless here in this world.

Remind me, O God, to live more simply
and that "here" is not my home.
Remind me, this day, to travel lightly
as I come homeward bound to you.

Monday of the Fourth Week

The story of the prodigal son also contains Jesus' theology of forgiveness and God's unconditional love. The returning hoe-boy might expect to see this hobo sign of a "judge" chalked on the gate outside his family farm. Yet the prodigal father loves lavishly and does not judge the sinful life of his barefoot, rag-attired son. Indeed, how easy it is to judge the poor, the homeless and those living on welfare as bums, as people who won't work. The father in the parable, however, has the eyes of God, about whom the book of Samuel tells us, "Not as humans see does God see; they see the appearance, but God looks into the heart" (1 Samuel 16: 7).

When you see someone dressed in rags who looks like a drifter and a beggar, do you judge that person to be homeless and mentally ill — or possibly a saint? An excellent Lenten hobo patron saint to assist in adjusting your vision of the poor would be St. Benedict Labre. Born in France in 1748, he lived at about the time of our American Revolution. He took the revolutionary Gospel message of Jesus seriously, so seriously that it seemed to have made him unfit for religious life! He went to the monastery and tried to be a Trappist monk, but was asked to leave. He then entered the Carthusians and Cistercians, but both times was again asked to depart.

Unable to find his place in any religious order, Benedict set out on foot, living in raw poverty, on a pilgrimage to various shrines throughout Europe. Benedict the pilgrim was by all appearances a dirty bum, unkempt, his clothing infested with fleas and lice. Upon reaching Rome, he spent seven years living as a homeless person, sleeping in the ruins of the Coliseum by night and by day praying ceaselessly in the city's various churches.

Benedict Labre's hobo life, however, did not end as a sad failure, for he was canonized and made the patron saint of beggars and the homeless! Who wouldn't love to attend church seated next a saintly person like Mother Theresa? However, who wouldn't move to another pew if a living saint infested with lice and fleas sat down nearby? While odor-free and flealess statues of Saint Francis of Assisi or Saint Benedict Labre might inspire you, their real-life presence might have a different effect — since they'd smell from not having bathed in months or even years.

So too, it is easy to reject today's poor and homeless, who may physically resemble these saints of the poor. Though readily shunned, however, these poor may be as dear to the heart of God as was Benedict Labre. God's eyes see beyond their dirty, flea-infested outer layers and deeply into their hearts and the gardens of their souls.

May I practice, O God,
the holy skill of non-judgment toward the poor,
approaching both the rich and poor as one blinded by love.

Tuesday of the Fourth Week

The Lenten roadside is greening, coming alive in the season of spring. Long ago the poetic love ballad, the Song of Songs, acclaimed that springtime spirit:

> Hark, my lover, here he comes, springing across the mountains, leaping across the hills. My lover is like a young stag. For see, the winter is past, the rains are over and gone, the flowers have appeared on the earth and the song of the dove is heard in our land (Song of Songs 2: 8-12).

God sings such a lover's song whenever and each time you turn around, repent and begin your journey homeward, even if you have only strayed slightly from the straight and narrow. While your life may not be as excessively wasteful as the prodigal's in Jesus' parable, strive to make your loving as excessively generous and prodigal as the father's.

Not only is spring in the air, romance is also on the wind during these Lenten hobo honeymoon days. While a honeymoon image may still seem strangely inappropriate for these purple days of the middle of Lent, at one time these were lovers' days. Lenten romance was alive in Germany, Austria and the Slavic countries, where it was customary to announce wedding engagements on the fourth (or *Laetare*) Sunday of Lent. These were also lovers' days because this was the traditional time for proposing marriage. In Ireland, the entire Lenten season was once traditionally the time for matchmaking, or *cleamhnas*. The older folks would customarily sit around during Lent, matching up their sons and daughters for weddings on Easter.

On this springtime Tuesday, recall that you are

traveling on a hobo lover's journey and not on some harsh penitential path of negative self-denial. Lent is a time when God seeks after you, when God is inclined to "mooch" your love — mooch being the hobo slang term for begging. (Hoboes of the late 1800s and early 1900s enriched our language with words like moocher, handout, punk, crummy, fleabag, flophouse and panhandler.) Rather than simply being a penitential season, Lent is the time for extraordinary, extravagant love.

Completely contrary to both common sense and today's religious practice, the father of the prodigal does not make his son do any penance for his failings and sins! In fact, he forbids his hobo son from having to mooch or panhandle, to beg to be forgiven, and even prevents him from reciting his list of sins and failings. More than great, God's love for us is prodigal, excessively generous. In light of such extravagance, these Lenten days shout out the question, "Is your response to God's love prodigal or pathetic?"

O God, inspire me today
to be prodigally generous in my love and pardon.
May I forgive without needing apologies
and pardon others without being asked.

Wednesday of the Fourth Week

Crummy is hobo slang for the crumbs, the lowest of leftover food, that is given as "handouts" to hoboes. These poor vagabonds have often been given only the crumbs and not choice bread or good food. One of Lent's holy duties is giving alms or charity, which sadly often ends up being crummy charity. When gifts are made to the poor, they are frequently only the crumbs of our middle- and upper-class surplus.

Politicians panhandle our votes by their promoting welfare reform. No one can argue against reforming the welfare system, for every system needs perpetual reform, whether it be educational, governmental or religious. Yet welfare reform for politicians often has little to do with improving the system or better serving the needy. Rather than renewal, welfare reform invariably means limiting the services and money given to the poor. Pray that you might have deaf ears toward those politicians who try to mooch your votes by playing on your greed and selfishness as they denounce welfare. Instead, pray for ears to hear the words of love and care for the poor that Jesus and the prophets spoke in God's name.

Recall that charity-justice is a twin word and that what you call "your" money is not really yours but only loaned to you by God. To the degree that God has gifted you with money, you are obligated in justice to share that gift with those who don't have basic necessities.

Is this week's hobo sign, "a well-guarded house," chalked

on your purse, billfold or checkbook? Is the money you give in alms what could be called "sweaty money" — money given reluctantly? Jesus said, "Give to everyone who begs from you" (Luke 6: 30). In less than a hundred years, his call to unconditional generosity was made conditional, dependent upon the merits of the poor who were begging. A Christian manual of the second century called the *Didache* said this of gifts to the poor: "Let the money sweat in the palms of your hands until you know to whom you are about to make a gift." As with other challenges of the Master, his call to generosity has been adjusted and diluted. For most people in most times it has been modified to read: "Don't give alms to those who are unworthy of them."

Was Jesus speaking poetically or playfully when he advised giving to all that beg from you? Before answering too quickly, remember his warning about the rich being like camels trying to squeeze their way through the narrow needle-eyed door of heaven. You may protest: But I'm only middle-class; I'm not rich. Carefully consider, however, whether that answer can squeeze through the needle-eye gateway of love.

As a Lenten practice, look closely at your average, middle-class, comfortable lifestyle. Now reflect on these words of Jesuit Father James Haug: "Some environmentalists now estimate that for all earth's citizens to enjoy the kind of comfortable, not lavish, middle-class lifestyle that you and I enjoy, it would take an additional three planets the size and quality of Earth to provide the adequate resources."

O God of a Big Heart,
let there be nothing crummy or small
about my love for you
and my charity-justice toward the poor and needy.

Thursday of the Fourth Week

Great saints of previous ages, in order to faithfully follow Christ, gave away all their money and possessions to the poor. Today, even if you give all you own to the poor, you cannot effectively help them until you become part of the process of changing — reforming — our social system. One powerful Lenten work you can do today is to promise at election time to vote to change the system. Other Lenten works might be to sign a petition for justice or to work for and speak out against any unjust practice in your workplace, marketplace, government or church.

We practice our faith by practicing charity-justice daily, striving to be just, fair and honest with others. Alms are often seen as *gifts* to the poor, yet every act of charity is at its roots also an act of justice. As we've already seen, one exercise of this twin virtue is the wholesome penance of being willing to pay your tax money so that those in need can live a better life. Social welfare programs allow you to assist the needy who would never find their way to your doorstep. Your tax money spent on aliens and the poor is another way to follow the admonition of Jesus to give in a way that does not let your left hand know what your right has given away.

"Those on welfare should go out, get a job and go to work." This is an age-old social reformer's cry that would be good accompaniment to the famous fifteenth century organ of French King Louis XI. Louis ordered the abbot of Baigne to invent a preposterous musical instrument to entertain the king's friends. The abbot good-naturedly agreed, and he gathered together a herd of pigs that ranged in size from large hogs to little piglets. He placed the swine under a velvet tent and arranged them in a row from the hogs with low, deep voices to the high-pitched piglets.

Then he constructed a large keyboard, by which each of the pigs was connected to a key by a wire that led to a small spike poised over its rump. When the king and his guests were seated, the abbot played his ingenious organ. The piercing pig squeals produced a recognizable song that delighted the audience. The concert was judged a great success.

"Those on welfare should get off it and get a job" is an old song, which, regardless of the pitch of the squeals, is easily recognized as an old song favored by those who live high on the hog. The majority of poor people are not bums who refuse to work; most want a decent job. Our charity-justice needs to extend as well to those who work but still live on the edge of poverty. For society isn't willing to pay unskilled workers a "living wage" and instead gives them only a "minimum wage."

Contemporary life is a worldwide webwork of workers, both hidden and visible, from cafe kitchen help to checkout clerks, from factory workers to those who farm the land. The clothes you wear and the food you eat come from that sometimes-invisible webwork of workers. Even if they are not physically present in your day-to-day life, being concerned about their working conditions and welfare is central to our call to charity-justice. Not to be genuinely concerned is to be sinfully blind and deaf. This is the season of repenting. If you have been mute to the needs of the struggling poor or have been singing that old song denouncing people on welfare as you join your voice to those in King Louis XI's hog organ, then consider repenting and changing your song. Sing a new song for justice toward all with the same passion proclaimed by Jesus and the prophets.

Open my eyes and heart, O God,
to the needs of the poor and poorly paid. May I do all I can,
wherever and whenever I can, to promote justice for all.

The Lenten Challenge — To Keep Falling

Two people were hiking once on a foggy day, and one accidentally fell over a cliff. The person on top of the cliff shouted down into the thick fog, "Are you all right?" From deep out of the fog came the voice of the one who had fallen, "Yes, I'm all right."

"Are you sure," shouted the one on the top of cliff, "you don't have any broken bones?"

Again out of the fog, only a bit fainter, came the response, "No broken bones."

The hiker on the top gave a sigh of relief and said, "Well, then, can you climb back up here?"

"No, I can't," came the reply, "I'm still falling."

The challenge of Lent and of every day is to keep falling — in love, that is. The central focus of these forty days, and of your entire life as a disciple, is to live out the great commandment to love God with all your heart, soul and body and your neighbor as yourself. Expressing such an all-consuming love is the sole reason for intense prayer, generous almsgiving and all the disciplines of Lent and your spiritual life.

Falling in love is a wondrous experience that is both intoxicating and spirit-liberating. Few break any bones in such a fall, even if a broken heart is a real risk. Yet, there is a universal rule in the gravity of love: All who fall in love sooner or later stop falling. Not all of us fall out of love, but who among us doesn't at least lose the passionate desire to invest his or her self completely in loving a spouse, a friend or God?

The paradox of heaven's gravity is that as long as you are falling in love with God, you are actually ascending a ladder into the Divine Mystery. Check your direction and position today to see if you are ever ascending in a continual falling in love. Or are you instead resting on some comfortable rung on the ladder of love? Each act of loving God is an act of climbing upward, whether the act is expressed in deep prayer or by sharing your goods with the least of God's family, which is the same as gifting God.

Lent is a profoundly powerful season; it is much like an escalator that assists the ascent to God. Like the gravity-free environment of a retreat, the activities of Lent — prayer, charity-justice and spiritual growth — lift us up escalator-like. Such an ascent can at times even make us light-headed. The first escalators, called "inclined elevators," were installed in Harrod's, London's very posh department store, in the early 1900s. Some store patrons almost fainted as they were carried upward on the moving steps. To remedy the shock of the unfamiliar sensation, Harrod's served all those who arrived at the top of the escalator a shot of brandy to help calm their nerves.

If you wish to ascend to God at such a rate that might make you faint enough to want a shot of brandy, plunge into falling in love with God with all your heart, soul, mind and body.

Friday of the Fourth Week

 Is there anything *fishy* about the degree of your love for God? Does that colorful hobo word, *crummy*, describe your prayer and your love of God? The way we spend our time, our energy and our bank accounts says much about what we love. Do you give God only the crumbs of your time and yourself? Crumbs may be usual fare for tramps, but when was the last time you threw a feast of your time and love for God?

If you abstain from meat on this Fish Friday, is it a sign of sorrow and repentance? And is your repentance an expression of sorrow for some character flaw or for a failure to respond generously to God's love? The more you love someone, the greater will be your sorrow when you cause that loved one pain. True sorrow for sin is not so much about breaking a law as it is repentance for having caused pain to your beloved. And if you ask, "How can I possibly hurt God?" recall the words of Jesus: "Whatever you do to the least of my brethren, you do to me" (Matthew 25: 45).

As a prodigal daughter or prodigal son who is serious about being homeward bound, could you say, "O God, I've not been a very good lover. I've broken your great commandment — not the sixth one about sex — but the first one about loving you with all my heart, soul, mind and body. But I'm willing today to work at keeping the commandment better." If you're willing to work, then you're not a bum — for as the old saying goes, "A hobo works and wanders; a tramp doesn't work and wanders; while a bum drinks and will not work and wanders — but not far enough."

Reflect again today on the homeward bound attitude of the prodigal son, who only considered himself worthy to be a slave or hired hand at his father's house. As you are traveling heaven-bound, is your attitude like his? Do you consider yourself worthy only to be the lowest worker in God's house? Would you be pleased to be but a lowly servant waiting on the needs of the saints? Are you willing to simply work in heaven's kitchen or serve by sweeping floors or doing odd jobs as a groundskeeper in the Garden of Paradise?

"Lord, I am not worthy" is not only a prayer before Holy Communion, it's a prayer to pray at heaven's gate. It was the prayer of the prodigal, who knew he failed to love his father and his God. With how much honesty do you pray that prayer before you come to Holy Communion, or do you come like a tramp or panhandler looking for a handout?

The word *panhandler* puts the above question into focus. It combines the Spanish word for bread, *pan*, with the gesture of a hand reaching out. Pious panhandlers are those who ask for the bread of the Eucharist while at the same time are unwilling to do the hard daily work of loving and forgiving that Jesus expected of his disciples.

Lord, I am not worthy, for I love you with but half my heart.
Lord, I am not worthy, but make me worthy by your healing love.

Saturday of the Fourth Week

 As this fourth Lenten week concludes, we can easily be tired of our efforts at reform — and eager for Lent to end. The hobo sign on this Lenten Saturday means, "Don't give up." Let it speak to you as now, more than ever, you invest yourself in your Lenten works and disciplines, intensifying your prayers and your efforts to be a saint.

The prodigal vagabond son surely must have seen this hobo sign on fences as he made his way home. For regardless of any misgivings, he continued his homeward bound journey. Don't give up: If you are truly sorry for your shortcomings, you can trust that God will give you more than a handout when you finally get home. Trust, if you are truly sorry for your poverty of love, that God will greet you with the lavish prodigal love of the father in Jesus' parable.

Throughout the parable teachings of Jesus, God's love is generous. It is given equally to those who have labored long and to those who only show up at the last moment. Yet this divine prodigal love might be resented by many hard-working, decent Christians. Like their patron, the homebody brother of the prodigal, they would see no problem in having the hobo sign, "a well-guarded house," posted on their homes and church doors. The brother of the prodigal is the patron of the guardians of Holy Communion as they judge who is unqualified to receive Christ. Such Communion guards forget that they too are guests at the Lord's table, and it is impolite for a guest to say whom the host may or may not invite to the table. Every parable is a mirror; so, in one way or the other, each of us can see ourselves in the bitter homebody brother in the prodigal parable.

Today, Saturday, is the traditional day when parish churches offer opportunities for confession in the Sacrament of Reconciliation. If his parable of the prodigal was intended as a teaching on the proper formula for pardon, didn't Jesus forget something important? It seems the father forgot to give his son some penance or punishment for his many sins. Instead of penance, the father gave orders for a grand party! In his teaching parable Jesus proclaimed the good news of a God who was not a judge but a great lover.

How sad, then, to see on the doors of a house of God the hobo sign for a well-guarded house. A far better hobo sign for any church would be the hobo sign of a cat, which means, "Here will be found a generous woman." How wonderful if that sign could be the sign of Holy Mother Church! Yet don't forget that you are the church. The church is the people of God, and all of us together are the church. What kind of hobo sign would your family members, friends and  co-workers mark on the fence outside your heart?

O God, by my renewed daily prayer, worship, almsgiving
and care for your poor, stir up my enthusiasm
into a fiery zeal to express my love for you.

Fifth Sunday of Lent

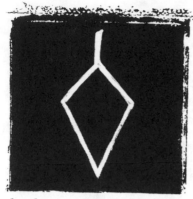 Scrawled in chalk over the temple wall near where Jesus is teaching in today's hobo honeymoon Gospel story (John 8: 1-11) could have been this hobo sign: "Be prepared to defend yourself." Angry at Jesus' having called them hypocrites and challenging their authority, the religious leaders set a trap to shame their enemy from Galilee.

Jesus is absorbed in teaching when the pious Pharisees drag into the circle of his disciples a woman caught in the act of committing adultery. The woman, who is "guilty as sin," is the bait in their trap, which is actually a trap within a trap. Jesus' enemies request his wise judgment on what should be her fate. If she is judged guilty of the sin of adultery, the Law of Moses required that the woman be stripped naked and her hair cut off; then both she and her illicit lover were to be stoned to death. The skull and crossbones sign — usually symbolizing death or danger — now is written large, if invisibly, on the temple wall above the spot where the woman is lying in shame.

For a conviction in the sin of adultery, the Law of Moses required the testimony of two eyewitnesses other than the woman's husband. Since they drag into their pious kangaroo court only the woman and not also the lover with whom she was caught sinning, this judgment scene stinks of a sting operation. This shamed woman is really but the cheese in the Pharisee's trap to get Jesus.

If Jesus is compassionate and says she should not be stoned, it will be construed as breaking the Law of Moses.

If he says, "Stone her" according to the Law of Moses, then he will violate Roman law. As of the year 30, no one in a country occupied by the Roman army could impose the death penalty, and John's Gospel implies that this law is in force. So Jesus is in a trap, the purpose of which is to show Jesus to be a hypocrite! He has told a beautiful story about forgiving in his parable of the prodigal son; here is a real-live prodigal daughter of Israel — how shall this real person be treated?

Jesus' enemies could have scrawled another hobo sign on the temple wall, the sign for a judge! This third sign today challenges the integrity of Jesus as a teacher. The spies of the Pharisees surely would have informed them that Jesus frequently taught his disciples never to judge others, and now he is being asked to judge another. The hobo sign for a judge looks like the kind of coil used to spring a trap, symbolizing the intent of this shameful lynching party of pious Pharisees.

Is the hobo sign for a judge chalked not on your fence but on the wall outside your heart? In this Lenten season of sorrow for sin, the act of judging others is a sin worthy of true repentance. Jesus forbade it. So, examine your conscience today to see how frequently this ugly sign has sprung up in your life.

O God, heal my endless itching
to be both judge and jury of others' deeds.
Seal my lips with the cross of Christ
so that they will never speak judgment.

Monday of the Fifth Week

 Jesus cleverly escapes the trap set by the Pharisees in John's Gospel by reversing the roles of who is guilty. In the process, he also reverses the meaning of the sign of the skull and crossbones. The Jewish Law required the eyewitnesses of the sin to be the first ones to cast stones to kill the guilty person. So Jesus invites the stone throwers to step forward, saying, "Let the one who has never committed a sin cast the first stone" (John 8: 7).

One by one, the jurors all depart, since none of them is sinless. As Jesus escapes their trap, he also rescues the bait, the shamed woman. Doing so, he gives another meaning to the death sign of a skull and crossbones, the same meaning it has in the language of the hoboes. It is now the sign of a healer. Wherever hoboes chalk this sign on a fence, it means, "A doctor lives in this house. Stop here if you're sick, and you will be healed."

The woman caught in adultery needed a doctor to heal her of disgrace as well as her sin. By refusing to condemn her, Jesus works one of many between-the-lines Gospel miracles, in this case healing the woman of her guilt and shame. You too can easily work such healing miracles if you discipline yourself to abstain from judging others. Long ago, not simply Fridays but every day of Lent was a day of abstinence from meat. You can likewise make every day of the year a day of holy abstinence by refraining from judging others and yourself.

Jesus proves he is both an ambassador of God's love

and not a hypocrite as he practices what he preached in his prodigal son parable. By his great compassion he also shows that he is a religious outlaw, for as Tom Robbins says in *Still Life of a Woodpecker*, "Love is the ultimate outlaw." Lovingly, Jesus refuses to judge or condemn the woman for her sexual sin, compassionately placing the situation outside the sphere of the law. Refusing to condemn such immoral behavior would still be considered shameful and shocking today. Good Christians are usually expected to point out and then to condemn sin, to judge sin while loving the sinner. That may sound nice, but how can we love someone while shaming him or her?

Jesus' silence in this case of adultery is shocking to puritanical Christians, who are excessively outraged by sexual immorality. (Remember too that at the time of Jesus the couples' parents arranged all marriages. Naturally, many such arranged marriages must have been loveless ones.) As he raises the woman to her feet, all he says is, "Go in peace, and avoid this sin in the future" (John 8: 10). This absence of denouncing her sin is disturbing to Christians for whom the greatest commandment is the sixth. Indeed, the major reason for excommunication of the laity and the removal of clergy — or politicians — from office is for sins against the sixth commandment. No one is ever excommunicated and barred from receiving Holy Communion for exploiting workers, for being a slum landlord or for sins against justice. The church term, "living in sin," refers only to cohabitation outside of marriage and never to operating a business that exploits workers, never to refusing for years to forgive someone.

O Spirit of God, teach me what is truly offensive to my Beloved God.
O Spirit of Jesus, appoint me not a judge
but your ambassador of love.

Tuesday of the Fifth Week

We are given a real insight into God in the prodigal behavior of Jesus, who is excessively kind to a sexual sinner and so harsh on the piously self-righteous. He called them hypocrites for robbing God's poor while showing off by praying to God on street corners. How many Christian business men and women attend prayer breakfasts while being dishonest in their private lives and business dealings, sometimes paying their workers as little as possible while demanding as much work as they can squeeze out?

Yet Jesus says to each of us, "I do not condemn you, but from now on avoid this sin" (John 8: 11). Remember that Jesus was talking about the sin of adultery! Before you too quickly deny that his words are meant for you, consider that adultery is the act of being in the wrong bed, or in the right bed with the wrong person. Examine your life carefully as to your bedmates, even if the act of adultery is only in your heart.

Prophets like Isaiah and Hosea compared Israel's lack of fidelity toward God to the sin of adultery. On this Lenten Tuesday, reflect on your faithfulness to God: Do you have "affairs" with other gods with names like Money, Work, Status, Honor, Power or Success? If you are guilty of romancing and making love with these or other gods, Jesus says, "I understand; I do not judge, but avoid this sin in the future."

Sadly, the religiously righteous were blind to the good Jesus did: his healing of the sick, giving hope to the poor, offering acceptance to those who had been outcast and proclaiming the unbounded love of God. Instead, they focused on his minor violations of religious law, like curing the sick on a Sabbath day and associating with sinners and social outcasts. The religious right of his day was habitually guilty of adultery, for they were in bed with the Law. They prided themselves on their perfect external observance of the countless commands of the Law while at the same time exploiting the poor and neglecting God's great commandment of love.

Lent is a churchwide season of reform — each of us is called to participate in this season of conversion of self. Converts are not just those who will be baptized and received into the church at Easter time. You and I also are expected to be converts. Conversion calls us to change radically, to converts our lives into something else. If you have been a lover of another god, and if you worship that little god by giving it your heart, soul, mind and time — then let yourself be converted now. The Latin root word from which we get *convert* means, "to turn around." So today's hobo sign is a defaced street sign: the familiar U-turn sign with the red circle and slanted bar removed!

Help me, O God, to make a U-turn in life
and to stop loving other gods.
Inspire me to be a perpetual convert,
ever eager for ongoing conversion.

Wednesday of the Fifth Week

The Muslim mystic, Abu Hassan Bushanja, said, "The act of sinning is much less harmful than the desire and thought of it. It is one thing for the body to indulge in a pleasurable act for a moment, and an entirely different thing for the mind and heart to chew on it endlessly."

A faultfinder chews on others' sins and failings with the pleasure of a dog chewing on a big bone. Sin-chewers, such as those who presented to Jesus the woman caught in adultery, enjoy chewing endlessly on the sins of others. The reasons for such a strange diet are complex, but many of these "bingers" are perfectionists; they desire themselves, others and life itself to be faultless. Often these faultfinders are obsessive correctors. Like most obsessive people, such faultfinders are starving to be loved, and they feel that if they are always right then others will love them.

Those who are unable to love themselves, including their faults and imperfections, find it difficult to be compassionate toward others. Like charity, compassion begins at home.

Yet what a miserable diet it is to chew on faults and sins. Usually faultfinders are even eager to share their meals of others' faults or unacceptable behavior with anyone close at hand. Nor do they hesitate to share their plate of faults about the weather, room accommodations, food they're served or the quality of the service. In this sad sin-chewing diet, positive comments — if any are offered — are only for desert after the long main course of munching on the faults of others. Often, the most delicious feast for religious faultfinders includes chewing on the sins of the flesh. They love gnawing on others' sins of shameful passion, although they will quickly tell you they find such sins to be disgusting. Psychopathologists, however, have long known that sexual disgust is actually a form of negative fascination.

As we move deeply into this Lenten season, there is a risk that it can become a time for chewing on past sins which are served up again and again as a kind of holy hash. Instead of rejoicing that God has pardoned and forgotten your sins, you may be tempted to chew on this or that old sin from your past life. There's a tendency to say, "Forgive me, when I was young I committed this sin of . . . " as a rehashing of leftover confessions. As your Lenten work today, you might soak even your oldest, most unresolved issues in a private ritual of joy-filled gratitude that God has been so prodigal in forgiving and forgetting your failings.

If you must chew on sin, then choose a fresh one — one of your own — into which you can sink your teeth. Choose a sin that you know separates you from God or harms the fabric of your relationship with a loved one. And better than chewing on it would be to face squarely and honestly your failing, and ask for pardon. Then pray for the grace to abstain from such behavior in the future.

Spirit of Freedom,
liberate me from chewing on the sins of others.
Spirit of Love, inspire me
to compassionately love myself and others.

Thursday of the Fifth Week

Sadly, religion can encourage sin-chewing. It can also be the source of your feeling guilty for not feeling guilty. These last days of Lent are times for penance services and the confession of faults. These can be valuable rituals for reform and conversion when we need to seek pardon and forgiveness. It's unfortunate, however, that sometimes when we feel no need for reconciliation we are still made to feel guilty for failing to attend a penance ritual.

Perhaps some of that guilt is bred in the environment that surrounds parish communal rituals of reconciliation. Often, there's still an air of purple gloom, dominated by a stark cross, with sad-faced penitents who, after confession, depart solemnly from the service. Seeing Lent as a hobo honeymoon would turn these rituals of reconciliation into the joyous celebration of a welcome home party. If the parable of the prodigal is how God welcomes back those who have sinned, should that not be the pattern for religious reconciliation? In that parable, the father refused to let his son chew on his past sins by confessing his prepared penitential list. Instead, the father embraced him and led him into a joyous homecoming feast.

Whether or not you attend a communal penance service this Lent, the place to begin your Lenten reconciliation is in your own household. There was once a tradition in Russia as Easter drew near: Before going to confession, the members of a household would observe a beautiful home ritual. Each would bow to the other members of the family, including the servants, and utter the age-old phrase, "In the name of Christ, forgive me if I have offended you." The ritual response was, "God will forgive you." Consider the profound healing effect such a ritual of anticipating sacramental absolution might have in your home. You could even extend such a ritual to those in your workplace! You could also make a creative addition to that age-old response: "God will forgive you…and I forgive you."

The hobo sign of a doctor says, "This person will heal, and if you are sick will care for you!" It's a symbol that should be chalked on the doors of your parish church and those of your domestic church, your home. This fifth Thursday of Lent also invites you to make the hobo sign, "will heal," your personal symbol and motto. You wear that sign when you refuse to judge others who have been married more than once, who are unmarried and have a child, who are dying with AIDS, who are unmarried but living together, who do not attend church on a regular basis or who are on welfare.

Becoming a person who heals is made possible because you have been healed, have been embraced by the prodigal father in a joyous welcome home party. If you then wish to practice your healing, you need to attend to some important principles. The first step to being a "doctor" is to look carefully at what is immorality in the eyes of God and redefine your notion accordingly. Second step: Refuse to eat or share with others a diet of chewing on sins. Third step: Abstain from judging. Jesus refused to judge or condemn the woman caught in adultery since he knew heaven's principle of true conversion: Kindness, not punishment, changes behavior. In the process, Jesus showed he was not a hypocrite, for he lived his own teaching: "Judge not, and you will not be judged" (Matthew 7: 1).

O God of Mercy, may I live daily in the joy of your forgiveness.
O Divine Healer, help me work miracles of healing
by not shaming others.

The Amazing Power of Baptism

For those who are about to be baptized at this year's Easter Vigil, these are days of anticipation and prayerful preparation. That ritual of Baptism includes everyone present renewing his or her own baptism. For many, baptism is an unremembered event of infancy. So this Easter act of renewal can be a declaration of an adult desire to become a new person, even if we can't remember the feel of the waters of rebirth.

Since this is a large communal renewal, it easily can become a hollow ritual, devoid of a significant religious experience and so lacking in far-reaching consequences. The key to making the renewal of your Baptism a significant climax to this Lent lies in your personal preparation. In the coming days, begin to anticipate that renewal so that you can bring to the Easter ritual a true commitment to live out your baptism as a new person in Christ. The act of being baptized — when the old person dies and is raised up out of the waters a new person in Christ — is more than just an entrance rite into a church. A favorite story of mine may help shed some light on this rebirth:

> Years ago there was a machinist who worked at the original Ford Motor Company plant in Detroit, Michigan. Over a period of years he had "borrowed" from the factory various car parts and tools which he hadn't bothered to return. While the management never condoned this practice,

nothing was ever done about it. In time, however, the "forgetful" machinist experienced a Christian conversion and was baptized. More importantly, the man took his baptism seriously and became a devout believer.

The very morning after his baptism, the machinist arrived at work with his pickup truck loaded with all the parts and tools he had taken from the Ford Company over the years. He went to his foreman and explained that he never really meant to steal them and asked to be forgiven. The foreman was so astonished and impressed by this act that he cabled Henry Ford himself, contacting the auto magnate while he was away visiting a European Ford plant. In his telegram the foreman described the entire event in great detail. Ford immediately cabled back this striking two-line response: "Dam up the Detroit River. Baptize the entire plant!"

Imagine the impact in your parish this Easter if those being baptized, and everyone renewing his or her baptism, would be changed as dramatically as the newly baptized machinist at the Ford plant! Instead of buying new clothes for this Easter Sunday, it would be more fitting to design a new you in which to celebrate the resurrection of Christ Jesus.

Friday of the Fifth Week

On this Fish Friday, abstain from chewing on your old sins, which God has long since forgiven. Abstain also from chewing on the sins and mistakes of others. One week from today is Good Friday, which commemorates the death of Jesus on the cross. On that Friday he shed his blood, which, as he said the night before at his Last Supper, would be poured forth "for you and for all, so that sins may be forgiven" (Matthew 26: 28). To continue to chew and chew on sins forgiven must surely grieve the Risen One who died that sins might be removed.

While the reflections on these past Lenten Fridays have focused on fish, today another traditional Lenten holy food is proposed: soup. The Irish, it is said, always have a pot of soup on the stove. This could be a good practice in your home the rest of this Lent, especially if it's a pot of stone soup. The ingredients for such a soup are easily found since we live in a new Stone Age. In the old Stone Age of Paleolithic times, the earliest humans used stones as tools and weapons. In the present Stone Age, stones are thrown in the form of accusations hurled with the malicious intent to mortally wound reputations of neighbors, clergy, politicians and a host of others.

So when someone hands you a stone of accusation or gossip about another's failing, drop it — drop it into your soup pot and make hobo soup. While associated with hobo stew, the food of hoboes and tramps, the original stone soup actually goes back to a sixteenth century story of a beggar.

In this old story, which is also known as the tale of Saint Bernard's Soup, a beggar comes asking alms at a mansion, but the servant at the door tells him that he has no food or money to give him. The beggar then says, "Can you at least give me a pot of boiling water, for I can make soup magically by simply dropping a stone in it." Being curious, the servant complies. The beggar drops a stone in the boiling water and waits and watches. After awhile he asks, "Could you give me a small potato or two, just to give it a bit of body?" The servant agrees and brings a couple of potatoes. So the beggar adds them and continues stirring the soup with great interest.

In due time he asks for a chunk of meat, then a carrot, followed by an onion or two, and finally a little salt and pepper, all the while stirring and tasting to see how the magic is working. The beggar at last says the magic has done its work and the soup is cooked, so he offers the servant a taste. The servant is amazed and declares, "A miracle! 'Tis a soup fit for a king. How delicious and magical to make such a soup out of a single stone!"

The next time you find a hot stone of scandal in your hand, drop it in your pot of boiling water, which you keep on the back burner just for such stones. Then add to this scandal stone a chunk of some good characteristic or quality the accused possesses. Next, slice up a memory of this person's kind deeds and perhaps a piece of his or her previous achievements. Stir your soup with a wooden cross as you add the spice of love, and slowly the soup of scandal magically becomes St. Bernard's hobo soup — fit for a king, the King of Kings.

Holy Redeemer, let me never cast a stone —
except into my pot of hobo soup.
Daily, help me to work the magic of making compassion soup.

Saturday of the Fifth Week
Silly Saturday

Tomorrow is Palm Sunday, and your Lenten hobo honeymoon is almost over. Tomorrow begins Holy Week, with its remembrance days of the passion and death of Jesus of Galilee.

Perhaps, as you look back on these Lenten days, you may find that the many demands of your home and work have tended to eclipse the good intentions you made on Ash Wednesday. If this has been the case for you, dedicate yourself today to investing yourself as completely and prayerfully as possible in Palm Sunday and Holy Week. Once, long ago, Lent was only observed for the seven days of Holy Week! Know that you have this rich, age-old tradition upon which to build your week of weeks. Even if you feel satisfied about your Lenten works, plan to make this Holy Week the best of all your weeks this Lent.

To spend this week as a personal retreat will mean moving your prayer and spiritual needs to the top of your list of priorities. You may feel silly asking to be absent from work in order to attend religious services that will help you invest yourself in the sacred mysteries of these days. Your practical-minded associates and friends may call you silly if you sidetrack the usual concerns of your life to make next week a homebound retreat. As a result, today has been named *Silly* Saturday as an overture to *Holy* Saturday, one week from today.

The day from which that blessed Saturday gets its special title, Good Friday, could also be called Silly Friday, since silly comes from the Old English *saelig*, which means, holy, blessed or saintly. We see this in an old English carol that spoke of Jesus as "the harmless, silly babe." Silly, which once carried the sense of being harmless and peaceful, in time came to mean weak and then foolish. Indeed, saints are silly, their behavior often appearing as foolish to others: loving their enemies, never returning evil for evil and giving to all who beg from them. Yet, while saints may be silly, they are not foolish.

If you decide to be countercultural and spend next week as a holy week, you may find it helpful to playfully rename the saints: Silly Francis of Assisi, Silly Joan of Arc, Silly Thomas More, and so on. Call yourself Silly Sally or Silly Sam as you desire to invest yourself deeply in the sacred mysteries of Holy Week. As you waste your time in such religious foolishness, you can strive for true silliness and blessedness.

The masters of the silly, clowns, frequently are dressed as poor, ragged hoboes and tramps. The key to the success of clowns as silly characters is that they simplify complicated human behavior. The great American clown Emmett Kelly's ragged hobo character, Weary Willie, wears a hangdog, sad expression as he stumbles around, unable to perform the most simple of tasks.

In the book *Clown*, Emmett Kelly said of himself, "I am a sad, ragged little guy who is very serious about everything he attempts to do — no matter how futile or how foolish it appears to be. I am the hobo who found out the hard way that the deck is stacked, the dice frozen (loaded), the race fixed and the wheel (of fortune) crooked, but there is always present that one, tiny, forlorn spark of hope still glimmering in his soul, which makes him keep trying."

On this eve of Holy Week, fan that spark of hope into a flame as you try to make this coming week the holiest of weeks in your year.

O Lord of Clowns, make me silly enough
to embrace my cross with love as I join the silly parade of saints
dancing behind my beloved Jesus, the Kings of Fools.

Palm Sunday

"Return to the Land of Your Soul" is a contemporary homeward bound chant that could accompany the prayer of every devout Jew at the Passover Seder when he or she says, "Next year (I hope to celebrate) in Jerusalem." For almost three thousands years for a devout Jew, to "return to the land of your soul" has meant to return to Jerusalem, the site of God's temple and David's royal city. And today Jerusalem is a holy home city not only for Jews but also for Christians and Muslims.

On this Palm Sunday, whether you live in San Diego, Boston or Kansas City, you can symbolically return to the Holy City as you accompany Jesus in his triumphant palm procession up to Jerusalem. Paradoxically, he enters this holy home city as the prodigal prophet who will face the anger of his elder brothers — the Pharisees, priests and scribes.

On this Sunday that celebrates Jesus' triumphant entrance into the Holy City, you will be given a palm branch. It is a sign that you are one of his companions going up to Jerusalem. In the long tradition of union IDs, your palm branch is a type of identification card proving that you are a Lenten hobo pilgrim. The term *hobo* first appeared in print in 1889 in the state of Washington, referring to migrant workers and lumberjacks. These hobo-migrant workers carried union cards to prove they were no bums looking for a free handout.

Instead of a hobo chalk sign, this week's palm sign is a simulated IWW union card. By 1912, the IWW, the Industrial Workers of the World, classified hoboes as card-carrying migratory workers. Forming a large part of the IWW labor union, hoboes would show their red IWW union cards to railroad employees as proof that they were working people, and so worthy of a free ride on a freight train. Their IWW union card also became known as a "pie card" or a "meal ticket," since housewives were much more likely to feed them if they knew the hoboes were migrant workers and not idle bums.

Over these past weeks, you have been homeward bound as a Lenten hobo pilgrim, and finally you will receive your union card in the form of a green palm branch. Like the "green card" given to aliens to show they are legal workers in the United States, so your green palm branch can be your verification that you are a pilgrim Lenten laborer. Your palm can be proof that as a Lenten hobo you have been a forty-day migrant worker who has labored at deepening your love of God and others. If you have been faithful to your disciplines and resolutions, then Lent has been work — although, hopefully, a work of love and joy. This labor is especially significant and challenging since you live in a secular society so lacking in tangible support for the hard work of reform. Today, you have a right to carry your palm with dignity, for you have earned it.

Beyond their use at worship on this Sunday, blessed palm branches can be valuable allies in your spiritual life. The following page will offer a few suggestions — to which you may wish to add your own — for using your blessed palm.

Blessed Palm, be a sign that I am a true pilgrim of the Cross. Be the green badge of a believer in the victory of the Resurrection.

Suggestions for Using Your Blessed Palm

1. Cut off a small piece of your blessed palm and carry it in your billfold or purse as you would a union card. Beyond Holy Week and Easter your piece of palm can be a reminder that you are a homeward bound hobo and a reminder to live a more simple life.

2. Pin a piece of your palm to the sun visor in your car or truck. It can remind you as you travel that all roads lead to the land of your soul. Your piece of palm can inspire you to use your vehicle as a rolling hobo hermitage for reflection and prayer.

3. Place a piece of your palm over your bed to remind you that if you die in your sleep your bed will be a bridge to the gate of paradise. Let it inspire you to fall asleep in peace with all people, secure in the knowledge that you are homeward bound.

4. Place a piece of your palm on your desk, tape it to your computer or make it visible wherever your workplace happens to be. Let it help you remember that whatever your occupation, it is really only a hobo part-time job, since you are homeward bound to God.

5. You may also wish to set aside a small sprig of each year's palm branch to be placed in your casket. A small sprig of palm could be pinned on your burial clothing or placed in your hands as a sign that you have been a martyr-witness to the faith. In Christian art throughout the ages, the palm branch has been a symbol of those who have given bloody witness to their faith. Palm branches are also signs of victory, and in the book of Revelation the saints in heaven are holding palms as a sign that they now share in the victory of Jesus Christ. A piece of blessed palm in your coffin, then, can be a most appropriate symbol of faith in the power of the Resurrection.

Lenten Honeymoon
⊗tra Hobo Prayer

I will go up to the altar of God
    to sing songs of gratitude,
for God gives joy in youth,
    joy in middle age
and the greatest joy in old age.

I go joyfully up to God's holy altar,
    not in the chains of obligation,
bowing, foot-dragging dreary, to do some duty,
    but to dance drunk in gratitude
before the Source, the Fountain of Joy.

Thank you, O God, for theftproof joy
    and ageless idealism.
Thank you for the joy of work
    well and honestly done,
for the easy yoke of obligations
    that are embraced out of love.
Thank you, too, for the joy of wisdom,
    gleaned from a glossary
of many mistakes and errors.

I will go up to the altar of God
    who gives joy in youth,
in middle years and in old age;
    I will go to God, the joy of my death.

Palm Monday of Holy Week

With each night of the final week of this Lenten honeymoon, the moon grows ever closer to its spring-Passover fullness. A good evening prayer for this Monday of Holy Week would be to go outside and listen to the moon. While seemingly silent, this special moon sings — for those with ears to hear — the same song she sang in Egypt to the Hebrew slaves: "Return to the land of your soul." About 1290 B.C., as the full moon made the night as light as the day, those rag-tattered slaves and migrant laborers heard her haunting call to depart from Egypt homeward bound to the Promised Land.

In that first Holy Week, Jesus knew his real work was not that of a village craftsman-carpenter. It was not even to be a teacher and preacher of the Good News. His real lifework was to go up to Jerusalem to die! Yet, profound was his belief that his beloved God would not allow him to be a prisoner of death and decay. The message Jesus gave to his disciples about his approaching death was always accompanied by his message and promise of life after death.

When he told them he was going up to Jerusalem to die, his brave disciple Thomas boldly said, "We will go and die with you!" (John 11: 16). That brave intention of Thomas, Simon Peter and the other disciples quickly disappeared when Jesus faced his brutal torture and death. Their belief in Jesus' promise of life after death became like a hobo pie card, and for the apostles it had turned into "pie in the sky." (It's interesting that this expression for any empty wish or promise was made popular by hoboes.)

In 1911, the rallying song of the IWW — the International Workers of the World, nicknamed the

Wobblies — was taken from a poem by Joe Hill.

> You will eat, bye and bye,
> in the glorious land above the sky,
> work and pray, live on hay.
> You'll get pie in the sky when you die.

Over the entrance gate to the original palm procession in Jerusalem, perhaps a sign should have been posted that read, "No Bums Allowed!" Of those who followed Jesus in palm-bearing triumph up to the Holy City, how many were only interested in being on the winning side and cheering a hero? How many who accompanied him had any intention of taking up the painfully hard work of suffering and dying? How many were willing to embrace death and so witness to their belief that his promise of eternal life was no "pie in the sky"? How many of those who were at church yesterday on Palm Sunday are "the church" today? It's easy to *attend* church and difficult to *be* church, to daily labor at the challenge of living out the Gospel.

The almost full moon of this spring Holy Week sings to you, "Return to the land of your soul." Siren-like, it calls you to follow the new Moses, Jesus — to be exodus homeward bound to the land of your soul. Heaven is the Promised Land, and those who believe in the promise of the Resurrection make that promise their heart's desire.

Spirit of Courage, inspire me to be
a true follower of the Crucified One.
May I be willing to follow him, the Risen One,
all the way to the land of my soul.

Palm Tuesday of Holy Week

By your labors to observe your Lenten disciplines, you can look honestly upon your green palm as your union-card proof that you are no bum on the road home. Christianity, like all religions, has its share of spiritually lazy members who refuse to do the hard work of justice-charity, compassion and prayer. How many Christians come to Holy Communion looking for a free handout? How many fail to show up for the work of reforming society and only appear for a free ride from the church at times of funerals, weddings and baptisms?

See your palm branch as your hobo union card, and know that the work of your union is, indeed, union — the labor to achieve unity. This season of Lent has been no solitary religious experience, even if it has been a very personal one. You have been part of a great multitude, a company of Christians of various denominations who have made this spiritual journey of renewal along with you. Your union work begins with striving for a loving comm*union* with God, the One from whom you've come and to whom you're returning. It is a daily striving for comm*union* with Christ, our Teacher and Suffering Servant. That work includes a movement toward unity with all who are in Christ the Risen One — which is all peoples and all creation.

In these days prior to his last sharing of the Passover meal with his disciples, many of Jesus' thoughts must have been upon the unity of his little community after his death. He expressed his desires for their unity so beautifully at that final meal when he said, "... that they may all be one, as you, Father, are in me and I in you... so that they may be one as we are one" (John 17: 21-23). This plea for unity is Jesus' last will and testament to his disciples. This plea for a perfection of unity among his followers, he said, would be a sign to the world that he, Jesus, had been sent by God.

After two thousands years of failing to respond to his dying request, disunity among Christians is more than sad; it is the greatest scandal of Christianity. It doesn't take a prophet to predict that the twenty-first century will demand that the world become a comm*union* of nations working for the same goals. The failure of banking systems in one part of the world now profoundly affects the economy in all countries. Air travel now easily allows for peoples of all races to visit one another's lands and cultures. Global satellite communications and the Internet have created among the peoples of the world what once happened only at the village well. Such cultural developments challenge religion, and especially Christianity, to assume prime leadership in working toward world unity. Yet many religions are still unwilling to work to end divisions among themselves unless it is on their own dogmatic terms.

Dedicate yourself on this Holy Tuesday to be a true union worker who labors ceaselessly for comm*union*.

Holy Spirit of Union,
help me make unity my daily and lifelong work.
Inflame me with a passion for communion
till we are all one in God.

Wednesday of Holy Week
Spy Wednesday

 Scrawled boldly above the doorway of this day are two hobo signs, the first of which means, "dishonest man." This fateful sign is observed in the Gospel for this Wednesday, the recounting of Judas' betrayal of his close friend, Jesus, to his enemies. In Ireland, this dark day popularly became known as Spy Wednesday. For, like a spy, Judas gave secret insider information about where and when the temple authorities might find Jesus alone so he could be arrested quietly.

Before Jesus experienced the pain of his scourging and crucifixion, he felt the stinging pain of betrayal by a friend, one whom he had invited into his inner circle of close associates. You may know something of this kind of pain if someone in whom you have placed your trust has betrayed you. Such a Judas-like act can take various forms: It may come in the violation a confidence shared with another in secret, the breaking of a commitment through divorce or some other desertion in a time of need. In whatever way you may have experienced it, allow that memory to soak deeply into your prayers and thoughts on this Spy Wednesday.

Even more devastating than being judged a hypocrite is to be called a Judas. May today's reflection on the pain of Jesus' betrayal so deeply influence you that under no circumstances would you become a Judas-friend. Regardless of the temptation, pledge that you will never betray a friend.

The second of this day's hobo signs means, "Danger, unsafe place." This equally fateful sign is etched in other places besides these holy days of Jesus' passion and death. Practice seeing this hobo sign on your bed, on your car or over the passenger entrance of an airplane you are boarding.  Death is always an unsafe and dangerous place, so you will be tempted, as was Jesus in the Olive Garden, to flee from harm's way. The easiest escape route from death is to deny its possibility each time you drive an automobile, fly in a plane or even fall asleep at night. Denial is another word for flight, and just as Jesus did not turn away from his approaching death, do not deny yours!

In this week dominated by the death of Jesus, find confidence in your long labors to make the kingdom of God a reality for yourself and those around you. As a hobo in life, be a living witness to the reality of another life by refusing to invest everything into this brief life. Heaven is no "pie in the sky." Joe Hill's poem, "The Preacher and the Slave," is about the empty pious promises given to the oppressed and those heavily burdened by hard labor. "Work and pray, live on hay, you'll get pie in the sky when you die," is a preacher's promise to honey-sweeten life's pains and the suffering of those deprived of justice. Yet your final home/destination is no "pie in the sky."

To return to the land of your soul implies that your real home is, indeed, that original soul land. While we may not have any specific memories of existence prior to our birth, we do have deep feelings for a place that feels like home. We have feelings of never being fully "at home" anywhere, never being fully satisfied with anyone or anything in this life, a perpetual yearning for "something else" that will bring us to true completion. Every time you experience these feelings of incompleteness, you might think of them as memories of that land of your soul from where you came and where once all was perfect and complete.

*Haunting voice of discontentment, rather than a cause of sadness,
be my holy bell-beacon leading me ever homeward bound.*

Lenten Honeymoon
⊗tra Hobo Prayer

From that vast ocean that is you, O God,
   my heart can only sip a drop
without bloating to the point of explosion.

From that blazing sun that is you,
   my flesh can only endure a ray
without being charred into cinders.

Blessed are you, for you give yourself to me,
   in tiny droplets of the sea
rather than the vastness of the ocean —
   in a single yellow sun ray
and not in the nuclear furnace of the sun.

Blessed are you, for my eye and mind can encircle
   only so much glorious wonder.
Gracious are you to lovingly come to me
   in doses of holiness I can embrace.
More wholly other and awesome are you
   than anything I can know, feel, sense or see.
You are my Source and Beloved Destination.

Holy Thursday

Homeward-bound Jesus, fully aware that he had come from God and was returning to God, knew the hour had come for him to leave this world for home. Great was his desire to show the depth of his love for his disciples at his final meal. So he took bread and said, "This is my body. Take and eat." Then, raising the cup of wine, he said, "Take this cup, each one of you, and drink from it, for this is my blood, the blood of the new covenant to be poured out for all so that sins may be forgiven" (See Matthew 26: 26-28).

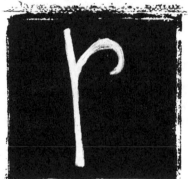 The hobo sign for Holy Thursday says, "Stop here if you are sick, and you will be healed." The Eucharist meal of Jesus is holy medicine for life's sick hoboes, a bread and drink that heals. The final Passover meal that Jesus celebrated with his friends was also a medicine to cure amnesia, the sickness of losing one's memory. The annual Hebrew holy meal of remembrance includes these words: "Eat and drink, and remember." Remember that once you were aliens, migrant workers and slaves in a foreign land. Remember that you are God's hoboes — a pilgrim, wandering people that is forever homeward bound.

By saying, "Do this in memory of me" (Luke 22: 19), Jesus made his last banquet the first of millions of messianic banquets to come. Sadly, that memory meal also began millions of battles among Christians about the precise meaning of the words of Jesus at his Last Supper: In what way does Christ come to those who keep the memory — fully in flesh and blood or only in some symbolic way? Christians are sharply divided over the meaning of the language of a holy meal that was intended to unite us!

The late Jesuit theologian Edward Kilmartin gave a fresh perspective to questions concerning the Eucharist. He said that we miss the point if the question asked is: "How does Christ becomes present to us?" rather than asking, "How do we become present to Christ?" Kilmartin said, "The movement is not from the historical event of the cross to us; the event is not withdrawn from its historical context and made to come to us. Rather, we go to the event, are made present to it."

"Do this in memory of me," said Jesus. The Greek word for remembrance, *anamnesis*, is the name given to the prayers in the liturgy that follow immediately after the words of Jesus over the bread and wine. More than recalling some past event or someone's name, *anamnesis* has the deeper meaning of "gathering together," gathering that which has been scattered and divided. The Jesus meal was meant to bring healing forgiveness for sins and also to be the medicine that heals the world's painful divisions, that gathers together what has been divided.

As Jesus gathered with his disciples, what was going on around the table of that Last Supper? Along with his male disciples, we know that Jesus' mother and his women disciples accompanied him up to Jerusalem, since they were present at his crucifixion. Were they absent from this very significant final meal, as it appears from all the artistic depictions of it? If those women disciples who had shared in his public mission did not also share in his last meal of meals, then his Last Supper, at which he prayed that all his disciples might be one, was the scene of a cruel and painful division.

While first century Near Eastern eating codes did not permit women and men to eat together, Jesus frequently set aside public and religious codes of conduct for the higher code of love. Is it possible that the first healing of divisions by the mystical food and drink of the Last Supper was the uniting of men and women at the table of the Lord? Apostolic writings report from the very beginning of the early church that men and women shared equally in the Lord's Supper. If Jesus did not himself replace the old, rigid code of table companionship with a new one, then who among his apostles would have dared to begin such a countercultural novelty?

And what was going on among his male disciples who gathered at table with him for this Passover meal? While they were individually deeply bonded to their Master, weak were their communal bonds among one another. They seemed endlessly engaged in petty feuding about whom among them was greatest. Jealousies divided them from one another, and especially from the apostle John, who was the favorite friend and beloved disciple of Jesus.

Surrounded by this splintered group of disciples, Jesus took the bread and wine and said, "Eat this bread and drink of this cup" and filled the food and drink with himself. As, one by one, his disciples ate and drank, were their eyes opened? As they ate and drank, did they re-member — did these separate members become the single body of their beloved master? The history of the early community of his followers reveals how much they became fused together as a single body, and their central gathering of unity was the remembrance meal.

The messianic banquet of Jesus was intended to remove sin as it struck deeply at the roots of the world's greatest sin-sickness: division. Holy Communion with him was meant to heal humanity of its discord created by competition in the marketplace, on the sports field, in politics, religion and the family. The medicine-meal he created was to heal the Body divided by negative attitudes toward sexual differences — heterosexual and homosexual, married and unmarried — to heal the divisions of social classes, races and nations.

Two thousand years after that Last Supper the plague of painful divisions continues to exist, and the most heartbreaking is the separation among his own disciples. That disease dissects the One Body, creating *sectarians*, a word that means narrow-minded and bigoted persons. Sectarians see their way to God as being the only way and consider those of other religions and sects as inferior or even diabolic. Each time Jesus' memorial meal is celebrated it presents an opportunity for those who are divided to be reunited as they remember who they are — the Body of Christ. Communion is the great memory of the land of the soul, the state of a profound unity shattered at birth, severed as one enters the world.

 Jesus said that only the sick come to see a doctor. On this Holy Thursday, present yourself to the Doctor if you are separated from the Body by various attitudes, assumptions or beliefs. As with this hobo sign of a doctor, all healing begins with an acknowledgment that you are sick and require healing. This awareness of needing to be healed is implied in the traditional prayer before Holy Communion. So if you find you are in need of healing, pray with devotion this variation of the classic prayer: "Lord, I am not worthy to receive you, for I have separated myself from your Body."

Each time you prepare to receive Christ in Holy Communion, remember that the critical issue is not how Christ comes to you, but rather how you make yourself present to Christ. By making that Passover passage, you may find yourself in the middle of a miracle. A friend told me that Albert Einstein once said, "There are two ways to live your life. One is that nothing is a miracle. The other is that everything is a miracle." If you live according to that second way, then it is not difficult to believe in the awesome mystery of Jesus' gift to us in the Last Supper. And the natural response to such a gift is sheer gratitude and wonder.

On this holy night long ago, as the first full moon of spring rose over Jerusalem, all those gathered in that Holy City were reminded of the Exodus honeymoon in the desert. Jesus said that he longed with great desire to eat that final meal with his disciples. Tonight and each time you come to his holy meal, bring to it a great yearning to share not only with Christ but also with his present-day disciples. That desire is more important than any theological distinction about what you will eat and drink. Bring a great desire, a passionate lover's longing, to eat and drink of the blessed mystery meal. Then, as you remember, you will be re-membered in and by the love of Christ!

O Lord of the Feast,
make me ever present to the gift of unity in your holy meal.
May I live daily as though everything — everything —
is a miracle.

Good Friday

The symbol of this day, which it seems all of Lent has been leading up to, is the cross of Good Friday. The Catholic tradition of Good Friday worship includes a ritual of reverencing the cross. One by one, worshipers come forward to venerate a wooden cross, kissing it with affection. If you are unable to attend church today, you may wish to have your own simple prayer ritual of reverencing the cross as the instrument of your salvation.

A second cross symbol could be inscribed on the entryway to this Good Friday. As Jesus enters Pontius Pilate's garrison headquarters today, he might well have seen the chalk hobo sign of a slanted cross scrawled on a wall. This hobo sign of the painful overture to his crucifixion means,

"If you go into this place, you will be beaten!" Jesus, the prisoner, is escorted under guard to a place where he is beaten and scourged on the way to being a victim of Roman capital punishment.

The fish sign that has marked each of the previous Lenten Fridays also has a special place on this holy Friday. When his enemies tested him by asking for a sign, Jesus would only give them the sign of Jonah and the great fish. Like hobo signs, the fish was a secret sign. It was an undercover code used by the persecuted early Christians as a way to recognize one another. The letters of the Greek word for fish, *Ichthys*, formed an acronym for the title, "Jesus Christ, Son of God, Savior." Early Christians painted the fish on the walls of Roman catacombs as a secret sign for  the Eucharist and for their faith in Christ as Savior. Like the cross, the sign of the fish is a Good Friday symbol for the death, burial and resurrection of Christ Jesus.

The scribes and Pharisees disregarded the signs of Jesus' many miracles and good works, oblivious to his countless cures of the sick and possessed. Instead, they demanded from him a sign that he was sent by God. Jesus replied, "Only an evil, adulterous and unfaithful generation seeks signs. No sign will be given you except the sign of Jonah the prophet" (Matthew 12: 39). Rather than a stunning miracle, the only sign he offered was a parable they knew well.

In that ancient story, Jonah is called by God to be a prophet of repentance to his people's worst enemies, the Assyrians. Jonah has no desire to save the Assyrians and tries to escape from his missionary vocation by fleeing on a ship. The ship, however, is caught in a great storm at sea and is about to sink. The crew, believing someone on board has offended the gods, casts lots to find the guilty one. The lots point to Jonah as the offender, and he is thrown overboard. The prophet is then swallowed by a great fish and is held a prisoner in the belly of the beast for three days and nights. Finally, the fish vomits him out on the very shores of the Assyrian capital of Nineveh, and Jonah does preach reform to the dreaded Ninevites. From the highest to the lowest, these pagans put on sackcloth and ashes, and God spares them and their city.

No fish story, the Jonah parable was given to the Jewish people at a time when they were being urged to completely separate themselves from those of other nations, to have nothing to do with their pagan foreign neighbors and their religions and customs. When Jesus refers back to the story of Jonah, he is aware that he will send his disciples like new Jonahs to the pagan, gentile nations of the world with his message of repentance. Like the pagans of Nineveh, these gentile nations, more than Jesus' own Jewish people, will hear his message and reform their lives.

The sign of Jonah also has personal implications for Jesus. Like the prophet Jonah, he too will be swallowed up in the belly of the beast and on the third day will rise again. The Apostles' Creed alludes to this time of Jesus in the belly of the beast by saying that Jesus died and descended "into hell" (the new translation reads "to the dead"). Originally, "hell" referred to the abode of all the dead, which the ancients called *Sheol* or *Hades*. In the Middle Ages it also took on the old Hebrew notion of *Gehenna*, a place of torment and punishment.

Today, belief in hell has declined. Some view it as a Christian torture chamber created by religion rather than by God. They find it inconceivable that an all-loving and compassionate God would create such a place of eternal torment. Yet every major world religion has its form of hell. Islam believes in a hellfire that is seven times hotter than any earthly fire. In an even older tradition, Buddhism has its own collection of demons that torture evildoers. The Aztecs of Mexico believed that only three classes of people escaped hell: those who died in battle, those who were the victims of sacrifice and those who died in childbirth. The Norse Vikings believed that those who died a straw-death — that is, in their beds — could not escape hell, while those who died as heroes went straight to *Valhalla*, a place of eternal joy and feasting. Yes, hell is a global belief and, as such, deserves to be taken seriously and studied for its implications.

In the Gospels, Jesus of Galilee spoke of *Gehenna* as "a place of fire prepared for the devil and his angels" (Matthew 25: 41). That Jesus would affirm the existence of a place of hellish torment is logical since he was a messenger of God's justice as well as God's compassion. For the persecuted and oppressed of the world, hell can be seen as a sign of hope! Since all of us are responsible for our own deeds, if we are not made accountable here and now, then shouldn't there be some reckoning after death? If those who do evil to others, trample roughshod over the weak and exploit the poor escape punishment for their deeds both in this life and in the next, then God's justice is made into a mockery.

Jesus spoke of hell not just because it is a part of death but because it can also be part of life. The capital punishment execution of Jesus on Good Friday was certainly a hell on earth. Every execution by lethal gas or the electric chair is also a hell on earth. To experience the death of a beloved, to go through a divorce, to be imprisoned, to be totally or partial brain-dead — these are also forms of a living hell, ways of being swallowed up in the belly of the beast. The image of Jesus being swallowed by the great fish of death embodies the awesome mystery of God entering into the depths of human suffering. Through Jesus' descent "to the dead," God is submerged in the various hells of all who are swallowed up in the many forms of suffering and dying.

Good Friday is our principal day to reflect on the death of Jesus — and also on our own death. This day serves up an experience of final death. It is like being swallowed up in the darkness inside the great fish, in which consciousness and memory are extinguished, speech is lost and the fear of the unknown is overwhelming. Today, when you reverence with love the cross of Christ as the instrument of your salvation, kiss it as an act of accepting your death. Although you know not how or in what way death will come to you, you can still embrace it with faith and love as you pray to die heroically.

Jesus died no peaceful straw-death on his mat-bed in Nazareth. Rather, his was a hero's death, dying as he lived. As a wandering hobo hero, he had battled against the forces of evil, the oppression of the poor, the injustices of the powerful against the weak, the pious manipulations of those in seats of religious power. Good Friday should not primarily evoke sadness from us his disciples but, rather, courage. The desire to be heroic slumbers deeply within each of us. On this day of history's most famous and terrible death, pray for the grace to live heroically so you too may die heroically.

When Jesus descended into the belly of the beast, what happened? The Apostles' Creed says, "He was crucified, died and was buried. He descended into hell, and on the third day he arose again." That decent into hell was the supreme act of love. The Muslim Sufi mystic, Abud Yazid al-Bistami, said,

> What is this business of hell? On the Day of Judgment I shall certainly stand with the damned and say to you, my God: Take me as their ransom. And if you will not, then I shall teach them that even your paradise is but a game for children. If, Allah, in your prefect knowledge of things to come, you know that you will torment one of your creatures in hell, then I beg you let me go to hell and let my body take up so much space there that there might be none for any other.

Is that a description of what the hero Jesus did when he descended into hell after he had ascended his cross? Because he so loved each of us, did he fill up all of hell with his body? Did God love the world and all of us sinners to such a degree as to will our redemption by the death, burial and resurrection of Jesus? Good Friday is indeed good, wondrous, holy and awesome, and it is the doorway to Home for all homeward bound hoboes. One day you and I will follow Jesus through the door of death all the way Home.

See boldly scrawled on death's door the hobo sign with which this Good Friday reflection began, the Greek cross of equal sized bars. As this day draws to a close, reflect on the meaning of this coded hobo sign, "All is good. All is right." The sign of Good Friday has come full circle from an ugly cross to a good cross. Let this hobo cross affirm for you that your death — although you may dread and reject it with all your power — is "good." As a good cross, let  it be a sign that frees you to live in hope.

Holy Saturday *or* Tomb Saturday
Easter Eve

The fish sign is also upon this last Lenten Saturday, a busy day of anticipation and preparation for tomorrow's great feast of Easter. This is decoration day; the purple of Lent is removed from churches as they are now decorated in white and yellow for the Holy Mother of Christian feasts, the Resurrection of Christ Jesus.

Holy Saturday is a special day for those who will be baptized into the church tonight at the Easter Vigil service. They are preparing themselves today for a very significant event in their lives, preparing to become fish-like. Jesus required each new disciple to become like a fish and be plunged deep into the waters in the rite of Baptism. The Latin name for the baptismal font is *piscina*, which means, "fish pond." In the early church newly baptized Christians were called *pisciculi*, meaning "little fish," since they were now one with Jesus, the great fish (*Ichthys*). This Holy Saturday, as one of his disciples, see yourself as a little fish swimming in the giant pond of the secular world in which you live. Rejoice that because of your Lenten disciplines you will be better able, even in a small way, to be an example of the great fish, Jesus.

Homes are also busy places on this Holy Saturday as they are cleaned and prepared for tomorrow's feast of Easter. They may be filled with the delightful aromas of special dishes cooking and Easter deserts baking. Along with aromas, memories of the family traditions of this day can fill the air and enliven your heart. Within the lifetime of some of you reading this book are memories of what happened on Holy Saturday at the stroke of noon when all the difficult penances of Lent ended. The stark contrast of the Lenten practices and the joyful Easter preparations made this day all the more memorable.

Some may recall their family ethnic traditions for this most special of Saturdays, like taking decorated baskets of breads and foods that would be eaten on Easter morning to have them blessed at the parish church. Once this was a special fish day in Poland. To celebrate the end of Lent's forty days, village boys would hold a mock funeral to symbolically bury the dull Lenten dish of herring. With glee and playfulness they would bury either a dead fish or a wooden image of one as a way of saying good-bye to the tiresome penance fish meals of Lent. You can imagine the fake crocodile tears of the mourners at these playful Polish fish funerals. Inspired by this old custom, you may wish to create your own Holy Saturday celebration. Consider a mock burial of the "old you" — bury tokens of the old habits or negative behaviors you have changed by your Lenten disciplines.

If you created a sackcloth scapular as was suggested during the first week of Lent, you might consider creating a simple ritual for removing it on this Holy Saturday. Such a private, prayerful ritual of removing your sackcloth scapular one last time can be a sign of taking off the "old person," so that on Easter you may be clothed anew in Christ.

This is a holy day for rejoicing, since Old Death was buried along with Jesus in the tomb. Yet while Jesus rose from the tomb on the third day, Old Death did not! On this tomb day, you might also want to visit the cemetery where your family members are buried and place a few fresh flowers at their graves. This Easter Eve pilgrimage to the burial places of your family and friends, even if it is only made in your heart, can be a hobo journey-meditation in preparation for tomorrow's great feast and for your own passage from life to death to Life.

Jesus' fish sign of Jonah expresses our belief about what happens to us as we share in Christ's death and resurrection. In your death, something dies, but not you. Hope in Christ says that as your separate individualism dies, your personality and memories live on transformed. Your distinctive personal identity remains when you pass through the belly of the beast; it emerges in glory, one with Christ and the entire cosmos. A reflection of your personal Easter can be found in the writings of St. Paul: "God has put all things beneath Christ's feet and made him the head of the Church, which is his Body, the fullness of the one who fills the universe in all its parts" (Ephesians 1: 22).

After death, even as you are one with the Risen Christ and in communion with all matter, with the whole cosmos, you still maintain your personal way of relating to others. When you're in union with Christ, the part of you that dies and is left behind in the belly of the beast is whatever in life separated you from others and from creation. Death is often spoken of as a departure, a leave-taking from those we love. However, Henri Le Saux, a French priest and holy man known in India as Abhishiktananda, was fond of saying, "Who leaves whom?" If we believe — and so act — as if our dead loved ones have left us when they die, is it not really we who have left them instead? What you believe can either separate or unite you. So let your Easter faith unite you to all those you have loved who are now fully one with Christ, who, having filled all of hell, now fills the cosmos.

Edmond Dunn wrote of a priest colleague who would create heated discussions among his students by suggesting that their grandmothers or other relatives were not waiting for them in heaven! It's true that your holy dead are not waiting for you! They live in eternal time, a zone of no time and place, where all is one and all is complete. From that eternal time zone they are not waiting for you, they are present to you *now*. Rejoice in and with them, and make tomorrow's Easter Sunday part of your preparation to join them in eternal joy and glory.

May a blessed Easter and Holy Saturday Vigil be yours.

Lenten Honeymoon ⊗tra Hobo Prayer

Such an obscene expression: "to die" —
neighbors do not die, they pass on;
friends and family do not die, they pass away.

"Died" is an ugly period-word that closes the door
    with a slam, seals the tomb.
Yet in our "passing on" avoidance
    is found a mystical truth.

For death is the great passage,
    a passing beyond sickness
and the valley of disappointment,
    a passage through the womb of the tomb,
a passage over life's limitations.

Since death is for you, O God of the Passover,
    a voyage of returning,
a joyous triumphant homecoming,
    help me, the next time I'm told
that acquaintances have "passed on,"
    not to cringe, but to smile
and to say, "Ah, yes, they have indeed."

Easter Sunday
Feast of the Resurrection

White rabbits and not hobo signs are the abounding symbols on this Easter Sunday. However, just as there are anti-Santa Claus Christians at Christmas time, so too on the feast of the Resurrection there are anti-Easter Rabbit Christians. They see the rabbit as a disgusting pagan symbol of fertility, which has nothing to do with the Christian celebration of the resurrection of Jesus. Moreover, if a large white rabbit were placed among the various symbols in your parish church on this Easter Sunday, most of the congregation would consider it an inappropriate sign. Yet, Christian mystics have seen rabbits differently — even, surprisingly, as symbols of those who do God's will!

One reason why the rabbit acquired this holy image was because of its physical build. Since the rabbit has shorter front legs, it was thought to be able to run uphill swiftly and so elude its enemies. The mystics considered this ability as a sign of a predisposition to seek the higher things in life and to do God's will, which they saw as always being uphill.

Rabbits were once also common in Christian — and in other religious — art. Some medieval cathedrals have images of three rabbits running in a circle so that their long ears form a triangle — a symbol of the Holy Trinity. Among the Buddhists, the rabbit is a religious symbol of self-sacrifice, since a hungry Buddha was once fed by a rabbit that freely jumped into a pan over a fire to become his dinner. The rabbit is also a religious symbol among Native Americans. In some of their spiritual traditions, the little innocent rabbit is a trickster figure that outwits big bears and mighty buffaloes. The Christian application of this Native American image of a rabbit trickster takes only a small step — or hop — since Jesus' resurrection outwitted the powers of this world and the forces of evil. Similarly, let all the small and large rabbits you encounter this Easter be holy symbols of Christian virtues and beliefs and of Christ, the Risen One.

The rabbit can also be your mascot for the hobo honeymoon you have been traveling over these past forty days of Lent. Indeed, as some are determined to point out, the rabbit is an old symbol of fertility and passionate sexuality. While at first that image may throw us back, its symbolic meaning is most appropriate for the followers of the Risen One, those who are called to be passionate lovers of God and of one another. Each of Christ's disciples is daily called to be as fertile as a healthy fig tree or a robust rabbit in creating the perpetually new reign of God.

 On the first Easter morning, the rising sun revealed a sign chalked on the side of Jesus' tomb. It was not the sign of a rabbit but this hobo sign that means, "Be afraid." Such a symbolic warning of danger might seem more fitting for Halloween than for Easter. Yet fright, and even terror, was the first response of those women who came to the empty tomb of Jesus on Easter morning.

This same hobo sign was also chalked on the locked door of the upper room where the little band of disciples was hiding in great fear. It is written large across each of the Gospel accounts of that glorious first day of the week, the day of the resurrection. As Mary Magdalene is weeping beside the empty tomb early on that morning, we can see the hobo sign, "Be afraid," chalked on the side of the wall above her. Mary is afraid that the tomb is empty because the buried body of her beloved has been stolen away. In the midst of her tears, she sees someone nearby that she believes to be a hoe-boy, a gardener. She asks him, "Sir, if you're the one who has carried him off, tell me where you've placed him and I will take him away" (John 20: 15). The mysterious stranger has only to speak her name, "Mary," and she instantly recognizes him as her beloved Master. As she rises to embrace him, the Risen Hobo says, "Mary, I am homeward bound to my God and your God. Do not cling to me, for I have not yet ascended to God" (See John 20: 16).

Mary Magdalene is Easter's hobo heroine. Although once considered a tramp, a prostitute, she became a great lover of Jesus. The Master even proclaimed her to be a model to emulate, since her love was greater than her sins. Her love was not lukewarm, but sprung from the fiery furnace of a passionate heart that consumed her many sins. Mary Magdalene is one of the patron saints of this hobo honeymoon and a mystical model for all who long to love God with all their heart, mind, soul and body.

Easter is the feast of hoboes, a feast for all those who have come from God and are returning to God. So it is fitting that this great feast should suggest another source for the origin of the word *hobo*, besides the homeward bound civil war veterans or the hoe-boy sons of farmers doing odd jobs after having left the farm. The word "hooboo" comes from a Negro slave slang word that slowly became part of white working-class jargon in the early 1900s. In the folk tales of Africa's Gambia River basin, which was a major deportation point for the loading of American slaves, a hooboo was a wandering ghost. One folk legend of the hooboo told of a great king who had lost all his possessions and power through evil sorcery and was cursed to constantly wander about the country dressed in rags.

In another version of the hooboo legend, he was a great singer who had challenged wind demons to a singing match that required more yelling than singing. The hooboo lost the contest, and the wind demons punished him by stripping him of his fame and reducing him to wearing tattered rags and wandering endlessly. In all the versions of the folk story, the hooboo is condemned to wander the roads dressed in rag-patches of many colors, and forced to depend upon the kindness of good-hearted strangers for his meals. To this day in West Africa, it is considered good fortune to be able to help any poor wandering person — who is really the great singer or a great king in disguise.

The accounts of the Risen Christ are in some ways like these hooboo folk tales. When the Risen Christ first visits his disciples, they see him as a hooboo, a ghost of their disgraced king of kings. However, the Risen One whom they encounter is no ghost, not even a holy ghost. The Risen Christ is not Jesus returned from a near-death experience, and his body is not that of a resuscitated corpse. Unlike Lazarus, whom Jesus had raised to life from the tomb, Jesus will never again face death. When taken out of his burial wrappings, Lazarus was identified by his family and friends as Lazarus. However, the Risen One's physical appearance doesn't resemble Jesus enough for his disciples to recognize him. While now transformed and transfigured, the Risen Christ they are experiencing is mysteriously the same person they had followed and loved when he was with them. This mystery of the presence of the Risen Christ holds a great Easter gift for us, for it is good news both about our own death and our body after death.

Easter's sunrise promise is that after death, we also will have a glorified, a glory-filled, body. St. Paul, writing in his letter to the Galatians, describes both the body of the church and our risen bodies: "There does not exist Jew or Greek, slave or free, male or female. All are one in Christ" (Galatians 3: 28). Here on this side of death we have bodies with a national identity and with various social, racial and gender differences. In your personal Easter, like the Risen Jesus, you will be filled with the splendor of God and a fullness of humanity that is neither male nor female. After he had risen, Jesus became *the* Christ, entering into the fullness and completion of "humanhood" and Godhood. This is the Easter gift promised to you and to all in this life who are one in Christ. For those hoboes who believe in his promise, their homecoming after death is more than life after death, it is a fullness of life and personhood that is beyond our imaginations.

Rejoice today in such a glorious gift that is promised to you. Rejoice today in the boundless grace of God as you take pride in how your good works, prayers, fasting and almsgiving during these past forty days of your hobo honeymoon have helped open the doors to the rush of God's grace. On this Easter Sunday you can proudly chalk this hobo sign on the door of your home or apartment.

The hobo sign that closes this Easter reflection means, "very good." You are entitled to such a high grade. Even if you yourself do not chalk this mark, the Risen Jesus will do so, saying, "Very good. Well done, good and faithful servant."

Easter Monday
or
Emmaus Monday

Your Lenten hobo honeymoon began on Clean Monday, the Monday before Ash Wednesday, and it is fitting that it concludes on a Monday, Emmaus Monday. Once, Easter Monday was a holiday whose Gospel reading was Luke's account of the appearance of the Risen Jesus on the road to Emmaus. Two disciples walking in sorrow because of the death of Jesus are joined on the road by a stranger, who inquires about the reason for their sadness. In a sunset meal at that village, while breaking bread, the disciples' eyes are opened, and they recognize the stranger as the Risen Jesus. As two versions of the hooboo story were told yesterday on Easter, so today you can reflect on this second version of the Emmaus story:

> The Sabbath had ended, and on the first day of the week the apostles Peter, James and John, afraid that they would be arrested, fled from Jerusalem for their safety. At sunset, they stopped at a small inn in the village of Emmaus. Taking seats in the corner, they spoke in hushed voices about the death of their Master. A Greek slave woman came to their table and, while pouring wine into their cups, asked them, "Why are you men so sad? You look like you've lost your best friend."
>
> "Woman," Peter replied impatiently, "we have indeed, but that is no business of yours. Go, be about your work!"
>
> "Sir," the serving woman replied, "I too

know the great pain of losing a dear friend, and I also know the pain of a broken heart. But death is not the end of love!" Then, to their surprise, she lifted up a wooden drinking cup from their table, pronounced a blessing over the wine and said, "Take and drink, this is...."

John jumped to his feet, saying, "Master! Rabboni!" In an instant, the Greek slave woman vanished before their eyes.

Christ, the Risen One, as you read yesterday, is not a he or a she. Jesus of Galilee was indeed a man and fully male, but when the Holy Spirit released him from the belly of the beast, Christ became both the new Jonah and a new Joanna. Christ is Jesus the man now transformed into a divine person one with God. It is helpful to place the title of Christ before the name of Jesus when speaking of him after the resurrection. It is also easier to use the pronoun "he" when speaking of Christ. Yet, since his resurrection, Jesus is now fully human and divine, and so, as St. Paul's words would imply, neither male nor female. For believers in the resurrection, every road and every meal holds an Emmaus experience of the Risen Christ, who is present in strangers and friends, in women and in men.

 This Emmaus Monday was once a holiday on which people would take short trips into the countryside as a way to celebrate Easter and to honor the disciples' journey to the village of Emmaus. As an encore day of Easter, this holy Monday also has its own hobo sign, which means, "Go!"

On the first Easter morning, the angel messengers could have chalked this hobo sign on the great stone that had been rolled away from Jesus' tomb. They told the women, "Go now, and tell his disciples that he is going ahead of you to Galilee, where you will see him just as he told you" (Mark 16: 7).

The Risen Jesus echoed that command to his disciples: "Go into the whole world and proclaim the good news" (Mark 16: 15). "Go!" is the Easter commission for disciples of Christ in every age and time.

Go — and feed the hungry; clothe the poor.

Go — and house the homeless and today's hoboes of the world.

Go — and care for all in need, and you will be blessed with more than good fortune. For when you care for Christ the Hooboo, you will be blessed with the fortune of heaven itself.

Go — daily striving to see the Risen Christ in all: in friends and enemies, saints and sinners, in the kind and unkind; show your love for the invisible Christ in them.

Go — into the whole world with the enthusiasm of those old-time newspaper sellers, who stood on street corners shouting the headlines. "Read all about it: Death Has Been Defeated. Life Is the Winner!"

Go — most of all, in joy. Travel the road of life as a joyful hobo, daily doing all things with delight. Live in the joy of this Easter season, which is a joy that no sickness, loss or defeat can steal from you.

Go — and live in joy since that is the parting wish of Christ Jesus. At the Last Supper, Jesus prayed that joy might be the abiding gift to his disciples: "...that my joy might be in you and your joy might be complete" (John 15: 11) and again, "...I will see you again, and your hearts will rejoice, and no one will take your joy away from you" (John 16: 22).

This Lenten-Easter reflection book has contained many hobo, and other, signs. It has offered challenges for discipleship that are to be lived beyond the forty days of Lent. May it encourage you to let each day of your life contain deep prayerfulness and generous charity-justice, along with a fasting from all that is negative in your relationship to God and an abstaining from judging and harming others.

As you prepare to close this book, embrace one more life-challenge for the coming Easter days. Daily, regardless of the circumstances, go into the world bearing not a chalk mark but the charming mark of every authentic disciple of Christ Jesus: Joy.

Lenten Honeymoon
⊗tra Hobo Prayer

Hallelujah!
    Praise God everywhere
on Earth and in space.
All creation wildly applaud
    the Almighty One.
Praise God to the outermost edges of the universe
    and beyond.
Praise God, all you supernovas and supermarkets,
    all you mosques and marketplaces,
    all you cathedrals and cabarets,
    all you temples and tennis courts.

Alleluia!
Praise God with resounding cymbals,
    and with crashing markets.

Praise God, you powerful majestic pipe organs
and you New Orleans jazz bands.
Praise God, you circus carousel calliopes,
and all you castanet-clicking gypsy caravans.
Praise God, all you with dancing feet,
and all you with walkers and canes.

Hallelujah!
Praise our Great God of Ten Thousand Names.
Praise God, all you holy saints in heaven.
Praise God, all you haloless saints on earth.

Let everything that lives on the earth
and in the oceans and seas,
and in the sea of space,
praise the Life that is
and was and shall ever be.
Alleluia!
Alleluia!
Alleluia!